TEARS IN SILENCE

Memoirs of a Transgender Child

JODY DUNGAN

outskirts press

The book is not intended for young readers.

It contains descriptions of self harm and suicidal ideation.
Parents are strongly cautioned.

Table of Contents

Preface

This is not my story!

I know, it's a strange way to start an author's preface, but allow me to explain. This is not the whole of my story. This book represents one aspect of my past with a very specific focus. After reading this, you might have an impression of me that is far from the truth. Most people who know me, see me as happy, exuberant and fun-loving. I'm often humorous and silly, and rarely exhibit any signs of the trauma that once dominated my young life. People change, and I am not the sullen, sad child of half a century ago. This work represents an important ingredient in my life. But in the same way that garlic is not spaghetti or peppers are not enchiladas, this is not my story.

I began writing about my childhood at the suggestion of a therapist who specialized in PTSD. At the same time, my pastor also recommended this form of therapy as a way of dealing with my past. I was skeptical, but decided to give it a try. It turned out to be one of the most difficult endeavors of my life. But it was also one of the most healing experiences I've ever had.

When I first started, I found I could only write for an hour or so before succumbing to sorrow. I would write for an hour and then cry for three. I often put it aside and wouldn't write for weeks or months. I didn't enjoy remembering the pain and confusion of those years. Consequently, the completion of the book has taken far too long.

As time when on, I found that I could write more and cry less and so, progress began to replace stagnation and hopelessness. Something strange began to happen as I wrote. I began to sleep better and longer. For decades I rarely slept for more than four or five hours a night. I remember my excitement when I awoke one morning and found that I had slept a full seven hours. I also found that I didn't wake up in "fight or flight" nearly as often. I didn't understand why, but I was beginning to heal.

People who have suffered past trauma have a tendency to react in one of two ways. Each of these represent extremes and are very unhealthy. In fact, trying to cope with past trauma in unhealthy ways can be deadly.

One way we deal with unspeakable loss and sorrow is to fixate on it. It becomes the focus of our lives, and unfortunately plunges us into the "Woe is me." mentality. We can become trapped in the never ending "Victim" label. We may use our past as an excuse for bad behavior or try to solicit empathy from others in an attempt to "feel better." Unfortunately, when we constantly remove the dressing to show people our wounds, they never have a chance to heal.

The second way folks try to deal with profoundly unbearable memories is through denial. This was my chosen coping mechanism for decades. Even though I rarely thought about my past, it was beginning to take a subconscious toll. Instead of taking the "I'm a victim, feel sorry for me." approach, I shrugged it off as "merely a flesh wound." I was taught not to show fear, weakness, pain or any kind of vulnerability. The problem arises when the wound is never addressed. It can form an abscess where infection takes hold. Sometimes I exhibited OCD behaviors and unexplained crying. Depression was always a threat and sometimes I had angry outbursts brought on by the slightest things. I was never physically violent, but many of my loved ones had to endure my verbal "hardness".

This book was more or less my attempt at cleaning, dressing and medicating a wound that had never been treated and had festered for far too long. I believe I was successful. The healing was painful and slow, but my Psyche is in far better shape than it has ever been. If you should ever meet me, you will see victor not victim. You will see far more joy than sorrow and much more love than anger.

In order for my writing to have the intended medicinal effect, it was essential that I wrote with integrity, without minimizing or exaggerating my experiences. Having said that, it's important for me to mention that not all of the dialog of so many years ago can be recalled. Most of the names have been changed and even the years when certain events occurred were obscured. I did this to prevent any embarrassment to my real tormenters who have no doubt become different people or have died. I have truly forgiven them all, but I still needed to record the events, thoughts and feelings of my young life.

I can say that every incident mentioned in the book did occur and my representation of the events and conversations are as close to the truth as I can convey. I hoped that this would chronicle not only the things that happened, but the effect that such hurt had on my young mind and heart. I'm not sure I adequately communicated my internal struggle and confusion. I guess in the end, we can only truly understand others through shared experience.

I hope you find connection, empathy, love and faith through the pages you read. This is my offering to a world that too often refuses to understand. I sincerely hope you are not among the willfully ignorant. If my writing can help one child avoid the kind of trauma I experienced, then it was well worth the effort expended.

My story is not yet over. It continues to unfold in profoundly beautiful ways. I offer you a piece of my history, but please understand, this is not my story.

Night Visitors

HIGH ABOVE AN old mining town in the Colorado Rockies, a snowflake wobbled, swayed, and tumbled in the darkness. Slowly it worked its way toward the sullen lights and the white blanketed streets below. It was lit by the streetlights only for a moment as it passed through a layer of wood and coal smoke. Delicately, it came to rest on the rooftop of a shabby apartment building for only a brief second, then quickly turned to water and was lost to the darkness as it joined the slush around it. Here it ended its existence as a unique sparkling object of beauty, never to grace our world again as it vanished forever into the night.

I could see the storm from my bed as I watched with glassy eyes through the rusted, cast-iron, multi-pane windows. There was a well-lit cone of snow beneath the streetlight across the woods. I could hear the storm as it periodically whipped the snow into a frenzy and howled through the trees. I remained perfectly still as I listened intently to the breathing from the bed across the small bedroom.

It's not that the bedroom seemed small, to me. At that age, nothing seemed small. In fact, our 802 square-foot apartment was a fortress and the smallest of the two bedrooms was the inner sanctum for a seven-year-old. The fact that the bedroom was on the second floor was even more reassuring since it prevented access by window. I always felt safe there, which was more to the credit of my parents than anything else. They always created safe spaces for my younger sister and I.

The storm outside would occasionally whip the snow into a restless, dancing multitude of white spots. The wind constantly changed the sounds outside from low moaning to shrill screams and back. But tonight, safe and warm in my bed, I listened and waited. As each breath became softer, deeper and measured I knew my sister was already drifting into slumber. Soft muffled conversations and deep sighs could barely be heard coming from the other bedroom where my parents wrapped up an exhausting day in each other's arms. I on the other hand, was not anticipating sleep.

I must have looked like a toy soldier left carelessly on its back but always at attention in its plastic form. My liquid blue eyes opened wide as they surveyed the room trying to make out shapes with what little light reflected off the blowing snow outside. Eventually I would sleep, but I knew there was something that was going to happen first. I was expecting visitors, so I quietly rolled to my right side, faced the window and prepared for their arrival.

For the most part, they were neither wanted nor unwanted visitors. They were simply necessary. They were a reminder of how truly broken my world was, and how desperate and forlorn my young life had become. My little friends didn't come every night, but I always knew when they would show up. And tonight, I had no doubt they were on their way. So, I waited in the darkness, without moving and completely silent.

The quiet darkness was interrupted by loud banging and rattling from the steam pipes. I was annoyed more than startled by the noise. We had all become accustom to the loud racket the radiator made as well as the smell of hot wet iron. The boiler two stories down decided it was time for a burst of steam and the gift of naked heat to these poorly insulated rooms. I waited for the noise to subside before

　　　　　　　　　　　　　　　　　　　　TEARS IN SILENCE

I began listening again. It was important to know when everyone else was asleep. I waited and listened and soon knew that my visitors had arrived.

I became aware of the first one crawling along my left cheek. It hesitated as it reached the crease of my nostril, slowly traced a semi-circle and dropped with a small thud to the pillow under my face. The second one made its appearance on the opposite cheek. Barely noticeable, it ran across quickly and joined the other on the pillow. More showed up as I tried desperately to control my body. I tensed up trying to stop shaking as my guts churned and I felt my stomach rise into my throat. I stifled a moan and turned it into a long, broken exhale. There would be many more that night. I welcomed them. I invited them.

Here in the still, quiet darkness I cried. Here I was in the safe refuge of my bedroom and alone with the broken heart of a young child. At this time only, could I feel my sorrow and know there would be no inquiries and no probes into this profound sadness. I wept the way a young child does when there are no witnesses, no comforter, no resolution and no hope. There was simply the raw release that comes from letting myself feel the way I truly feel. Even the hopelessness I felt took a back seat to the task at hand. That task, that all important labor was to simply let it all go. Here at this time only, my young heart that had barely embraced the world a few short years ago, could bleed its tears onto the linen and never have to offer an explanation.

After what seem like hours, my exhausted body, salty eyes and wet nose merged with the soaked pillow as I took my turn and slept. In the morning, I would simply pick up the mantle, don the armor and put up the walls again. Then for a time, I could walk through the world and try to be who I was supposed to be, but never who I truly was.

The muffled sound of the alarm clock coming from my parent's room took my breath away as my heart accelerated. I could feel the blood sounding through my ears as the realization of the nightmare to come took hold. The room seemed frozen in the soft light filtering in from the snowy landscape beyond the window. The alarm clock was always one of the most horror filled sounds of my young life.

It wasn't that I was sleepy and didn't want to get out of bed like a lot of kids. In fact, I've always been an early riser. I wake up quickly and within a few seconds I'm completely ready to function normally. Years later I would discover that my ability to wakeup instantly is due to the residual effects of trauma. For decades to follow, I often woke up in a state of "Fight or Flight", with my heart pounding.

For me, the alarm was a loud battle cry and the herald of the approaching pain. I knew that in an hour, I'd be required to ready myself for school. Soon, the cycle of suffering would renew itself, as the cool kids, the not so cool kids, the bullies and even some of the teachers would take turns dishing out different flavors of injury. I remained perfectly still in that gruesome twilight.

Somehow the passing night had destroyed yesterday and given birth to today. But for me, there were far too many yesterdays that would never be gone. They had left a residue and a most terrible effect on a young child. After a few minutes of contemplation, I lifted the covers, swung my tiny legs to the left and planted them on the cold wooden floor. And so, commenced the daily ritual of breakfast, face washing, teeth brushing etc.

I'm not sure what others think about during mundane tasks such as these, but I was usually replaying in my mind the painful events of the previous school days. I reviewed them in a desperate attempt to try to understand why they had occurred and to plan to do things differently in the future. My whole life at this time was focused on survival. I would make a careful analysis of places, people and situations to avoid. I sifted through my memories trying to understand what I might have done differently. But in the end, I was left with the realization that there was little I could do to stop the dreadful unfolding of the day.

I often had to stop myself from succumbing to moments of panic when my heart began to race and I'd have to concentrate to slow my breathing. The jingling of car keys always told me that ready or not, it was time to follow my mother to the door and leave the sanctuary of the apartment.

The storm had lightened up during the night, but a few tiny snowflakes were still floating from a breathy grey, chilled sky. It was cold that morning which made the tires on the snow-packed street sound like Styrofoam being crushed. The sun was making a feeble attempt to shine, but was only able to manifest a small glowing circle slightly brighter than the surrounding clouds. It seemed like neither the sun nor the storm had the will to distract me from my fear and dread. The tires against the hardened snow groaned slowly past the fence at the end of the driveway.

Multi colored cracker box houses lined the street. I recognized some of the houses where my classmates lived. I was never invited inside, but I tried to pay attention to students entering or emerging from homes. By that, I could know which places posed the greatest threat on the days I walked home. There were days when nothing at all happened, but there was frequent enough bullying so that fear was my steadfast companion and despair hung over my life like the murky dishwater clouds that morning.

The rhythmic clicking sound from the turn signal told me we were almost there. As the school came into view, I swallowed hard and began looking for threats. Sometimes it felt like walking the gauntlet just getting to my desk.

Once the parents who were dropping off their children were out of sight, it began. The boys would take a direct approach by tackling, tripping or shoving me to the ground. I still recall the crunching noise as my face hit the crusted snow. It often ended with some vile label spewing from their lips. But sometimes, there were fist jabs or a few kicks just to drive the point home, though I never knew exactly what that point was.

Girls were almost more brutal, as they mocked the way I walked or rolled their eyes with musical chants they'd made up. But the absolute worst were the teachers. When they got into the act, it made the whole thing seem institutionalized, like the entire world had conspired to make my life hell. I couldn't help imagining God chuckling from heaven and approving of my punishment.

I didn't know what words like queer, homo or fairy actually meant, but I knew they were meant to hurt. These and other words darted out of so many mouths, like angry wasps. Each disparaging word carrying its own venom, slowly poisoning and destroying some of the most beautiful things inside me. Trust, openness, honesty and belonging simply shriveled under the weight of so much hatred and rejection.

Getting inside the school was fairly easy that morning. As I approached the double doors leading to the school foyer, I heard a voice on my right snarl, "good morning sissy."

I knew it was John, but didn't dare make eye contact. I found that making eye contact was a good way to draw unwanted attention and provoke the bullies. More than one attack had started with words like, "What are you looking at, you fairy." And so, in silence I kept looking straight ahead with my eyes slightly downward. As I cleared the big double doors, I heard whispering as three girls in my class began giggling at me. I walked on through the foyer, turned right and headed down the hall. As I entered the classroom, and exhaled in relief, I settled into my desk and relaxed a bit.

Another day had begun and I had been safely delivered to the hands of my abusers. Another day, not to cherish, but to simply survive. I tried to think about the end of the day, when once again I'd be home safe at the dinner table or in my bedroom. I wondered what my mom would cook for dinner. I imagined watching TV with my dad. But for now, I had to focus on getting through the day as safely and smoothly as I could.

As I took my seat, I noticed my body was starting to relax and unclench. I knew there was less violence while in the presence of the teacher, especially in the classroom. Even the teachers who had no empathy for me still maintained order and discipline in the classroom. I took a few breaths and then focused on the worksheet Mrs. Taylor

　　　　　　　　　　　　　　　　　　　　TEARS IN SILENCE

had handed out. The assignments were very easy to complete, So I had time to daydream. There was always plenty of time to wish and dream. Fortunately, there was also time to analyze and plan.

I finished the worksheet in about five minutes and turned my gaze to the window. As I looked out the huge plate glass windows on the left side of the room, the sounds of the classroom began to sound farther away and the scene faded as I found myself in a new setting. On this particular day I chose to remember, not daydream. It was not a happy memory. in fact, it was the most disturbing and painful memory of my life. It was the day everything changed and my world collapsed.

Address Unknown

IN THE SPRING of 1962, I was confronted with a problem of such horrific magnitude that no four-year-old could have understood. I don't remember what I was doing at the time. I was probably roaming through the house like a typical toddler. Perhaps I was carrying a toy or munching on a graham cracker. In any case, it must have seemed like any other day. I couldn't have known that my entire world was about to change drastically.

My aunt and her daughter, were visiting that day. My cousin was almost two years old, but wasn't quite potty trained. As I walked into the living room from the kitchen, I notice my mom and aunt changing my cousin's diaper. They had placed her on the top of a walnut television console which worked well as a changing station. I stopped to check out what was happening. I had seen my sister changed before and this was no different, or, so I thought. However, on that day, it must have been something inside me that was different. I don't know if my little immature neurons fired differently on that day or if I had just finally connected the dots as my brain developed. I was about to learn that gender is more than what I felt. There was a real physical difference between boys and girls.

As I watched, I thought, "Oh no, this isn't right." But as I stood there, a growing sense of horror accompanied the budding realization that things were not the way I thought they were. I knew my sister was a girl, I knew my cousin was a girl, and they looked the same. But I also knew I was a girl too. I knew it through and through, but I didn't look like them. As my young mind struggled to put it all together, I really didn't want to see the truth of what was in front of me. Finally, it dawned on me. "I'm a boy?", I thought, "How can this be?"

As my heart started to race and the room began to spin, I felt my ears getting warm and soon my cheeks began to burn. I thought I'd pass out, but I didn't. I began to feel very strange. I found myself looking back at the scene as if from a great distance. It felt as though I was someone else, watching me. I think this must have been the first time that I had ever experienced that feeling. It certainly wouldn't be the last. It scared me so bad that I quickly snapped out of it.

I ran to the other room and buried my face in the couch and began to cry. I wished I could have crawled into the crack of the worn, brown sofa. It stank of cigarettes and garage dust. The weave of the stiff fabric felt like sandpaper on my tender cheeks. I wanted to hide deep inside the sofa, and forget what I had just discovered.

A few minutes later, my mother entered the room. She gently sat on the sofa next to me. She placed her hand on my back and began to gently rub as she said, "What's wrong sweetheart? Talk to Mommy".

My mind groped to try to find the right words. I desperately wanted to tell her what I had figured out and how terrible it was. But in the end, at that age I had neither the logic to understand or the verbal skills to convey what had just occurred. So, in order to dispel scrutiny, and not wanting to upset her, I acted as though I was just pretending to cry. My relieved mother laughed, called me a little faker, kissed me on the forehead and left.

The decision to hide the issue would cost me dearly and eventually lead to decades of soul crushing loneliness. It was the kind of secret a child holds in their heart, waiting for the day when they could talk about it, but it never felt like the right time. I also had no idea how to explain this to my parents in a way that they would understand. I suppose I could have simply said, "I want to be a girl." But it was more than that. I really was a girl, even though my body indicated that I was not. As the days and years passed, it became harder to reveal.

The most difficult thing about all of this was that I didn't understand what was happening. I couldn't understand how God could let this happen. Why would God put me in a boy's body? I pondered. This didn't make any sense to me. I was terrified and hurting from the truth that I had discovered. It's one thing to experience emotional pain and confusion, but to have no understanding of why this had happened to me and what it meant was worse.

When we suffer alone with no one to share our burden, it eventually gives rise to despair. To have no one even know you're suffering is perhaps the greatest pain and the deepest loneliness we can experience. Such sorrow, isolation and despair should never be part of a young child's life. But for me, it was as if the sun, had been blotted out, and all that was left was a dull grey existence emptied of joy. No four-year-old should ever have to feel that.

Sometime after the devastating revelation, I finally thought I had figured it all out. I had seen cartoons where the stork got drunk and delivered a baby to the wrong family. There was one cartoon where a gorilla family received a human child and another where a mouse baby had been delivered to a cat family. "It must be something like that." I thought. But in my case, it wasn't a baby in the wrong household, it was a soul in the wrong body. There must have been a mix up of some sort and all I had to do was get in touch with God and let him know what was going on. I thought, "Surely, he'll fix this once he knows about it."

I wondered if there was some unhappy little boy out there somewhere who was in a girl's body, my body. I wondered if he was as sad as I was. I wondered what my real body looked like. I tried to imagine what color of hair and eyes my real body had. But I had no way of determining where this little boy might be. The boy in my body could even be in a different country. And of course, he would have different parents. I didn't want a new family. I loved the family I already had. I just wanted the body I was supposed to have. All I really knew, was that only God can fix something like this. And so, I began to pray. My prayers were often the desperate, pleading prayers of a young child in pain.

At that age, some prayers were part of being tucked in by my parents at night. Of course, they were the routine, repetitive and simple prayers a child says before bedtime. "God bless Mommy and Daddy". They included requests to protect and bless other close relatives. And occasionally a request to help a sick loved one. They always included some version of, "Please help me be good.", and ended with "Amen." This was followed by being tucked in and kissed on the cheek or forehead.

After my parents left, I'd very quietly get out of bed, kneel and beg God for a miracle. "Also, God, if you're still listening will you please turn me into a girl?" I whispered. "I'll do anything you ask. I've been really good. I've kept my room clean and always try to do what Mommy and Daddy ask. Please? Are you there? God?"

I prayed with the innocence and naivety of a small child. I made the most desperate plea to the God of my understanding and closed my eyes with the joyful expectation that in the morning I would wake up in the body of a girl. Night after night I prayed. I prayed until my knees were sore. For a time, I would wake up and put my tiny hand between my legs only to be met with disappointment. Eventually, I began to lose hope.

Jody? Jody? The distant voice was calling my attention back to the classroom. "Yes ma'am" I answered."

Softly she said, "You need to put your name on it." Her finger tapped at the top of the page, the only thing on the worksheet I had forgotten. She wasn't scolding me, just reminding me. She never scolded me. In fact, there was always something soft and kind in her voice when she spoke to me. She never said it, but something in the way she addressed me felt like she was saying, "I care. I see you, and I care. "She smiled and took the paper with her back to her desk.

A spit wad splatted against the back of my head and I wiped it away without really thinking about it. In truth, I "forgot" to put my name on a lot of papers. I hated writing my name, the same way I hated seeing my face in the mirror. They were reminders of who and what I was, and I was beginning to dislike myself very much. Anything that reminded me of me, was unwelcome.

My gaze was drawn back to the window once more and I returned to my younger self. This time I remembered things that had happened when I was a little older than five. Around this same time, my family was attending a Southern Baptist church. Every Sunday we'd put on fancy clothes and go sit on wooden benches to hear a man yell at us about God. I understand now that not every preacher sounds like that, but this one sure did, or at least that's how it sounded to me when I was five. I think it must have been one of those "Fire and Brimstone" preachers that people talk about. The church was usually cold and the emptiness of the room and the tall ceiling caused an echo that made things sound scary.

During these times, I tried to pay attention to the preacher simply because I needed to contact God to let him know what had happened. I tried praying to God. I tried praying to Jesus. Then one day the preacher explained that we needed to ask The Father in Jesus' name. "Wow! That's it", I thought, "Just ask in Jesus' name".

Now I had a new formula and I could hardly wait to try it out and get in touch with my maker. Well, the new prayer recipe didn't work either, but I persisted only because there was nothing else to try. I wondered if God could hear me, so I tried praying louder. Of course, because of the nature of the request, I didn't want to be overheard, so I did most of that kind of praying outside when I was alone.

After a while I gave up asking God for a miracle. I hadn't given up on miracles altogether, but I thought that maybe God was too busy to waste his time with just one kid. "Maybe he gives the small things to his helpers, like angels." I thought. Maybe God only gets involved with the big things like making planets and stuff. I didn't know the names of any angels, but that didn't stop me from asking for miracles. I just started asking other magical beings for help.

I had seen The Wonderful Wizard of OZ, and so the first person I turned to after God was a beautiful "Wish granter". I started asking Glenda, the Good Witch of the North for my miracle. When she didn't answer, I tried asking my Fairy Godmother which was something I had seen on Cinderella. I really felt good about contacting my fairy godmother. After all, if she can turn a pumpkin into a golden carriage, turning me into a girl should be easy. When that failed, I tried The Blue Fairy, from Pinocchio.

There seemed to be an endless procession of miracle makers and magical objects portrayed in fairy tales. I tried wishing wells, wishing on falling stars, wishing as I blew out my birthday candles and so on. I considered Santa, the Easter Bunny and the Tooth Fairy worthless in this regard. They didn't seem to do miracles, they just brought presents, eggs and loose change.

Anytime we were with my mother at a secondhand store, I desperately handled and examined every pot, pitcher or vase that looked like it could contain a genie. The more interesting and exotic the container looked, the more hope I had that I would soon have my three wishes. On and on it went, and the wish was always the same. The desperate wish I always made was to be a girl.

When none of these magical beings showed up to grant my wish, I assumed that I was the problem and not them. I always felt that I didn't deserve a miracle. After all, most of my life had been composed of social rejection and I really began to believe I deserved it. Why would I think these folks from the unseen realm would behave any differently? I sometimes imagined Glenda or my Fairy Godmother laughing at my request or turning away in disgust. I even thought that they might actually harm me instead of help me. I suppose, that deep down, I thought maybe I deserved their rejection. So many people had hurt me, that it couldn't be the rest of the world that was evil. It must be me, and I probably deserve to be hurt.

My mind drifted to another memory that happened around the same time. Not only did I have to deal with my internal conflict, but there was also an external struggle materializing. This was when the physical violence began. My father and mother were never physically or emotionally abusive. I'm so grateful that my dad was always even tempered and fair when it came to me. However, he never tolerated fear or weakness in his "son".

One day, shortly after moving into our new apartment, I was sent out to play. As I emerged from the porch of the apartment building and started to explore my surroundings, I encountered a threat. A boy who was years older and much larger approached me and shouted angrily, "Who are you?" We had never met before, but he seemed quite upset that I was there. "I'm Jody." I responded not knowing what to expect next.

He walked up to me and poked me hard in the chest. "If you're still here when I get back, I'm gonna kick your ass!" He then chased some other kid who was also larger and older than me. He tackled him and began to violently beat the poor child. Shocked and terrified I returned to the entry and climbed the stairs to the apartment. When I entered the living room, my father was reading a newspaper which obscured his face.

"What's up?", he asked.

"Nothing, I just decided I didn't want to play outside.", I responded.

His voice changed as he growled, "Don't lie to me."

I explained briefly what had happened, and waited for him to lower the newspaper and say something. He never lowered the paper, but issued the firm command, "Get back down there."

I didn't hesitate. Dad always demanded immediate obedience. I exited the living room once more, and trembling went down the stairs to await what was sure to be an unpleasant and painful encounter.

The enemy appeared on cue and approached me. He poked me in the chest once more and said, "Why are you still here?" "Didn't I say I was going to kick your ass?" I didn't make eye contact, but kept my head bowed waiting for the first punch, but answered, "Yes."

"Aren't you afraid of me?", he continued, the anger was rising in his voice.

Still looking down, I softly answered, "Yes, I'm afraid of you."

He responded with an even louder and more angry voice. "Then why are you still here?", he screamed into my face.

"I'm more afraid of my dad.", I answered quivering. He hesitated for a moment still looming menacingly over me. I closed my eyes, and I braced for my beating. What happened next took me by surprise.

"Well. Did you want to go do something?" He asked

I was shocked, but finally made eye contact. Stunned, I responded, "Sure." As we both went off to find something to do.

I've often thought about that day and wondered what had averted his wrath. I think he understood what it was to be afraid of a father's punishment. In truth, he most likely had far more to fear from his father than I ever did mine. Whatever else he was, he was also a child who feared his father. I'm certain that bullies do what they do because they've learned brutality from someone much older and stronger. Finding themselves faced with a menacing adult who injures, some children act out by brutalizing those who are weaker. This was probably his story and my honesty had spared me. But the reprieve from harm that day, did little to lessen the hurt from so many other bullies in the past, and the ones that were yet to come.

The sounds of the 2nd grade classroom rematerialized as Mrs. Taylor was handing out another assignment. I needed to work on that, at least for a few minutes. I had to draw lines between the words and the matching pictures. I quickly finished it and turned my head back to the window and began to think about God again. And once more, I left the classroom far behind. I returned to my memories of our church again, when I was a bit older, in fact, this memory had been only a year ago, at the age of six. This was a much darker memory which filled me with dread and underlined the sadness of the day. I remembered and angry preacher and the angry God he represented.

〜

AN ANGRY GOD

GOING TO CHURCH gave me more than new techniques to try to reach God. It also taught me about a thing called "sin". My childish understanding of sin was simple. Sin was something we did that made God angry. And sometimes he would punish us for it. Some sins were worse of course, but it all made God angry and we needed to apologize in our prayers to keep him from hurting us.

One Sunday morning, as we walked up to the church doors, mom held my right hand and my father firmly gripped my left, as they helped me "hop up" the stairs. I was getting a bit old for that, but they still indulged me occasionally. There were the usual handshakes and greetings that mostly took place above my head. Once in a while a man or woman would squat, welcome me and shake my hand. But that didn't happen very often. Adults were usually fine with ignoring small children.

My family sat near the front on the second row back, which was our usual place. The wooden pews were hard and cold and smelled of furniture wax that day. Once we were seated, my parents scooted closer, squishing me between them. This helped me stay warm in the poorly heated church. I could feel my father's comforting warmth looming over my left side and my mother sat close to me on my right. She had draped her coat over her legs to keep them warm. My sister, sat on my mother's lap sucking on a toy. The smell of burnt dust filled the chapel as the heaters tried to dispel the chill of the morning air.

The preacher was yelling again. His loud and assertive voice never scared me, but I always wondered what he was angry about. This day, the pastor spoke on homosexuality, and crossdressing. Of course, those were not the words he used, but it was the 1960s in a redneck mining town and he was always trying to scare us into being good.

I remembered part of one verse. It said that these people were an "abomination". I didn't know what the word meant, but I carried it around in my head for quite some time. It was obvious from the tone of his sermon that those people were in really big trouble with God. What I didn't understand at the time was that I was probably not much different from "those people".

The crossdressing part really concerned me, once I understood what it was. Of course, the King James Bible didn't make that easy for a child. But eventually I understood that God didn't want us to wear boy's clothes if we were girls and boys weren't supposed to wear girls' clothes. I didn't know why that would make God so angry but every time the preacher said such things, people sitting near us would shout "Amen." So, I believed it was true.

Everyone in church, including my parents saw me as a little boy. However, I knew that God knew the truth about me. He was looking down at a little girl wearing a boy's suit. To make matters worse, I was doing this in his church. All I could imagine was an angry bearded face scowling at me from heaven and saying, "How dare you enter my church dressed as a boy?" In fact, I had never been dressed as a girl. "So, have I been crossdressing my whole life?", I wondered. "Maybe, if my parents knew I was a girl, they might let me wear a dress to church, just to make God happy." How naive I was at that age to think such things. Fortunately, I kept silent and never brought up the idea.

For the first time in my young life, I felt the judgment and con-demnation of an angry God. I had seen more than my share of angry scowling faces, but I had always thought that God loved me and would help me one day. I was starting to have my doubts about that. I knew that the other kids hated me. I knew that some of the teachers hated me too. Now I had to worry about an angry god who might also hate me.

Weeks later I asked my older cousin what abomination meant. He was five years older and to a six-year-old, he was the "coolest" person I knew and appeared to my young eyes to already be an adult. I was nervous about asking him, but it felt safer than asking my parents. I didn't think he'd question me too much and it turned out I was right.

I must have butchered the word because he had a hard time under-standing me. Once it dawned on him what word I was asking about, he said it out loud to verify what word I was trying to say. When I heard the word spoken again, I said, "Yeah, that's it."

Then he asked, "Have you ever seen anything so gross it made you want to puke?"

I thought for a moment and remembered how my cousins and I had found a dead cat in an alley. It was gross enough when we found it, but one of them flipped it over with a stick. The insides of the cat spilled onto the ground revealing all of the vile things living inside it. Also, the smell was so bad that it made me pinch my nose and hold my breath.

"Yes", I answered, softly almost whispering as I began to under-stand how God saw me.

"Where did you hear that word?" he asked.

"At church", I responded, as he began to smile and chuckle a bit. I told him, "Thanks" and went to my room to sit and think.

I found myself despised and rejected by my peers, made to suffer social isolation, grief and unimaginable loss. But I always thought God was on my side and had my back. And now I believed God was against me as well. This was all pretty heavy stuff for a kid in 1st grade. I sat on the bed silently repeating the word "abomination" in my head. Pictures flashed through my mind as I repeated the word. I thought about the disgusting cat. I saw Images of angry boys beating me, my face in the mirror and of course a wrathful God watching from above.

This was the time of my life I stopped believing that I was a good person. I knew I couldn't change. I mean, how do you stop wanting the one thing in your life that you believe will make you happy? And yet, the evidence that I was evil had finally sunk in. I didn't want to be evil, but I was, or at least that's what I believed. At this time of my life, my prayers changed. I no longer prayed that God would make me a girl, I prayed that he would fix me and take away my evil desires. Finally, I quit praying at all, because I knew I couldn't fool God and I didn't want to be a boy.

After a while, as I sat there in dark reflection, Dad came in my room. "You want to go get ice cream?" he asked cheerfully. "Sure, I responded as I slid off the edge of the bed and onto my feet. That took the edge off my grief as we all headed for the truck. Sometimes we'd drive over to the local A&W for shakes or cones.

We owned a small green Dodge pickup back then, and all four of us sat in the single seat. My dad looked at me and rubbed my head as he smiled. "At least Mommy and Daddy still love me.", I thought. Then the most terrifying realization came over me. If God hates me and God is never wrong and he doesn't make mistakes, then in truth, I really should be hated.

And what about my parents? How embarrassing it would be for them if they knew what I was. I thought, "If they find out, they'll stop loving me too. They'll hate me like all the others." That realization choked my breath. I'd seen the anger and disgust on so many faces, I couldn't bear to even imagine that look on my parents' faces. I glanced up at my dad sitting next to me and scooted a little closer to him. "What if they find out I'm an abomination?", I thought, "I can never let them know about me." That day, I resolved to never tell my parents the truth.

The shame, guilt and fear that materialized around this secret made me feel like I had killed someone and buried them in the woods. I was certain that someone would find the body any day, and the truth would come out and destroy my family. Then I would lose the last good thing in my life. I would lose my parent's love.

What I didn't understand at that age was that I was destroying my life by isolating myself. People cannot be truly happy without friends, or at least someone to talk to. I was marching into a wilderness without any meaningful connection to people outside my family. Even the relationship with my parents couldn't be completely honest. I had to keep everyone out of my most secret and troublesome truths.

This was the day I threw the little girl inside me in a secret room and locked the door. And with that, I got rid of the only witness who knew about me. Well, God knew, but he wasn't being very talkative. And maybe if I pray hard enough and beg long enough, he'll change me.

The horror of remembering the feelings of those days, snapped me back to the classroom. My heart began to race once more. As I looked around, I was so afraid the other kids could read my mind or at least my face.

Morning passed with relatively little pain. There were the occasional hateful words like fairy, sissy and homo that other students mouthed silently at me. I was hit with a few spit wads in the back of the head when the teacher wasn't looking and even a rubber band shot from a few desks away. It left a red welt on my cheek, but faded a few hours later.

Unfortunately, noon was approaching, and leaving the classroom always posed a much greater risk, even if we were simply going to the lunchroom. The bell rang and Miss Taylor organized us in a line to lead us down the hall.

As I entered the lunch area and approached the registers, I was greeted with the usual sight of kids lining up and pulling out their punch cards or cash. The smell of cafeteria food was always welcome to a hungry child, as I tried to guess what we were getting that day. There were three lines and I always chose the line that looked the safest. This was based upon who was standing at the end. I quickly scanned the rows and picked the left one which appeared relatively safe.

After several kids filed in behind me, I began to relax a bit. Unfortunately, I was wrong to let my guard down. One of the nastiest bullies crowded in front of me which I allowed without complaint. I backed up a bit just to give him room.

I seriously thought about switching to a safer place, but we weren't far from the registers, so I convinced myself that it would be OK. I really should have switched lines because a few seconds later, he turned around and said, "Don't stand next to me, queer!" This was followed by a hard punch to the jaw. I heard that familiar cracking noise in my ears whenever my neck was twisted sharply from a blow to the face. I staggered from the line holding the left side of my cheek and jaw. I looked quickly for a place in one of the other lines.

Just then, one of the teachers monitoring the lunch area yelled at me, "Get in line Jody" The commotion must have caught her eye, but she didn't see the reason I was out of line in the first place. She forcefully grabbed me by the arm and placed me at the end of the middle one.

By this time, most of the other kids were pointing and laughing at me. But I was more concerned about the pain in my left cheek. I was worried that it might swell or bruise. Then there would have to be an explanation offered to my parents. By explanation, I mean lie. Usually, it wasn't hard to convince them I was running near a piece of playground equipment and slipped. I always tailored the lie to fit the location and type of injury. But I really hoped it wouldn't swell or leave a visible mark.

Eventually, I made it through the line and got my food. I sat down in the very crowded lunch room. As usual, hands appeared, quickly snatching food from my tray. I didn't even try to stop them anymore. It had proven to be a fruitless effort, and usually solicited violence of one kind or another. So, I just sat there hoping there would be something left when they finished.

I started to reach for the pizza as a large hand from the right claimed the main dish. When I saw who the hand was attached to, I quickly withdrew my protest. As I watched my favorite school lunch evaporate, my stomach wrenched with hunger.

Then I surveyed the damage. The cookie and pizza were gone but I still had my milk, green beans and some apple sauce. I ate as fast as I could and finished the dismal remnants of the meal.

After lunch, we were allowed to go outside for a short recess. The playground was always rough. I had been hurt more often and more severely when I was outside the building than I ever was inside the school. If I remained close to the teachers, they would usually pull the bullies off of me when they had me down. Unfortunately, I was so afraid of the other children, that I always tried to get as far away from the center of the playground as possible.

Being away from the crowd gave me better visibility, an escape route, and prevented boys from sneaking up behind me. Tragically, this location was far from the teachers on recess duty. So, when things went bad, I knew there would be no quick intervention. The teachers were usually busy talking to one another and often didn't notice when boys had me down kicking or hitting me.

It was better to have a safer location than to cling to the thin hope of a timely rescue. Recess ended, and on this day, nothing bad had happened other than being yelled at by the teachers for venturing too far away from the other students.

I returned to the classroom with my jaw still aching. I took my seat and immediately turned my eyes to the window and looked out to an approaching snow storm. It looked like it was crawling toward us over the hills north of town.

I wasn't really focused on the storm. I was concentrating on my breathing. When I began to feel the warm, swelling feeling around my eyes, and the familiar choking sensation, I knew I was on the verge of tears. "No!" I thought to myself. "I'll never let them see me cry". After a few minutes of slow, controlled breathing, I felt the urge to cry die down.

My desk was next to the elevated heater vents that often smelled of burning dust. Just beyond the heater was the huge plate glass portal into my memories and imagination. The outside world darkened from the dense storm clouds. This made the reflections of the well-lit classroom more noticeable, and the deepening twilight outside harder to observe.

As I settled back into the space, my own reflection caught my eye. I sat up strait and looked at the face mirrored back at me in the window. What I felt at that moment was hatred. I hated that face. I hated the person behind the face staring back at me. As the feelings of anger and despair filled me, I mouthed the words, "Stupid! I hate you!".

I realized at that instant how true the words felt. I think I had been waiting a long time to express self-hatred in such a direct way. Again, and again I repeated the words, "I hate you!"

I was startled when I heard Miss Taylor ask, "Who are you talking to, Jody?".

It was then I realized that she could also see my reflection. "Nobody, Miss Taylor." I answered. My voice came out broken and shaky, which immediately raised a look of concern on her face. I could tell that the other students were looking at us.

I turned toward the window and said, "Looks like a bad one."

"The storm?", she queried.

"Yes." I said, hoping the menacing clouds outside would draw attention away from me.

It distracted my classmates, but not Miss Taylor. She had read my lips and gently placed her hand on my shoulder and asked if I needed to talk.

"No ma'am." I responded, without making eye contact.

She walked on and continued handing out another worksheet. We all turned our attention to the assignment and got busy completing it. Occasionally, I'd look up at my reflection in the window. I didn't have to say it, the face in the window knew how I felt. But I gave myself the meanest most hateful looks that I knew how to make, but only when nobody was watching.

It felt strange to express such things even with a look. Hatred and anger were not in my nature. Even when I was being bullied, I assumed it was something I deserved. Afterall, so many people hated me. How could they all be wrong? These people were teaching me how to hate. I was learning to hate myself.

The dark grey clouds loomed north of us, but each time I looked up, the clouds had moved closer and had started enveloping the town. At the same time, something dark also began to take its place in my mind. Something so dark, that to talk about it makes people very un-easy. "I could get rid of me.", I thought.

As I stared out the window, there was only one question in my head droning over and over. The question, was, "Why?". Not "Why did this happen to me?", or "How does everyone know what I am?" or "Why do they hate me and want to hurt me?" or even, "Why did God make me this way?" Just "Why?", which encompassed all of them.

The last few months of the school year passed slowly. It felt like watching cold honey creeping out of the jar and onto my biscuit at breakfast. At times it felt like it would never end, but like the honey, I knew I simply had to wait and I'd eventually taste the sweet reward of patience.

As the days and weeks passed, the weather outside started to change. The nice, sunny days began to be more common and always lifted my spirits. This was especially true on the days when the hurt seemed un-bearable. I simply had to imagine the last day of school and my release from the sorrow of constant bullying.

The school year finally ended and once again I could let go of most of the fear, and stress of social interaction. The fact that school would one day return and darken my world stayed in the back of my mind. But it seemed so far away, that I could focus on the pleasures of summer and just play. All of the children loved summer vacation, but I think for me the happiness of those months of carefree life were especially joyful.

Unlike winter, summers were filled with colorful sights, strange sounds like frogs at night, and especially smells. Some days I went fishing with my family. On these outings I remember the wonderful smell of the water and the forests, but also the unpleasant odors of fish and bug spray. On many occasions we ate dinners in the woods and cooked over open fires. Hamburgers and Hot dogs were common and we never had to eat the yucky things like spinach or liver.

On an outing near Emerald Lake, my cousins and I were allowed to cook hotdogs over the campfire. We sat on the ground in the smoky air trying to roast our dogs to perfection. Papa had cut willow switches for skewering our hot dogs. He was careful to make sure to cut some of them small enough to be managed by our small hands.

The pine smoke always burned my eyes, but at least it kept the mosquitos away for a while. The tall dry pines all around us made cracking sounds as squirrels leapt through the trees and snapped small twigs or dislodged pinecones. In the distance I could hear the voices of other families on outings.

I remembered the explosion of color in summer. There were the various greens of the plants and trees, and the beautiful wildflowers that grew everywhere. Birds and other wildlife were abundant and filled me with wonder as a young child. Mosquitos were always present but I hardly ever noticed until I was covered in itching bumps. There were creams to stop the itching, and sprays to keep the insects from biting in the first place.

All of these fabulous scents and visions fill the memories of my tender young summers. But mostly, I loved the freedom to be by myself and alone with my thoughts and prayers. As harsh as winters in Leadville were, we were surrounded by forests, lakes and mountains on every side. Mountain summers were peaceful and glorious.

THE ECHOING DARKNESS

SUMMER EVENTUALLY ENDED and school began. I hoped that this year things would be better, but that didn't prove to be the case. In fact, bullying and ridicule continued, and in most ways, had only gotten worse. The boys had gotten older and stronger which increased the amount of damage they could inflict. This was also true socially, and the girls had become more vicious as well. It was almost like they had been taking lessons on how to make other kids feel bad about themselves.

Shortly after classes started, we were on the playground during recess. When I was invited to play with some of the boys, I was thrilled to be included. In fact, it was one of the few times I was ever invited to join anyone at any kind of play.

I had gotten a small bag of marbles as a gift for my birthday from Papa. They included several beautiful "cat-eyes" and one that looked like it had been made out of stone instead of glass. They were beautiful and became one of my treasures that summer. I had become quite good at the most popular marble games, including the one I was about to play.

This particular game started by drawing a circle on the ground and then everyone would donate a marble or two that were placed in the center. The object was to "shoot the marble" By holding it firmly cupped with the index finger and pop it out using the thumb. With enough practice I found that my aim was impeccable, but I often lacked the strength to knock the other marbles out unless they were close to the edge of the boundary line.

If you succeeded in knocking one of them out of the circle, then you kept it until the end of the game. Once all of the marbles had been claimed, the game ended. Then everyone counted the marbles to determine the winner. It didn't matter if you lost the game, since once it ended the marbles were given back to the original owner. At least that was the way it was all summer playing with my cousins and some of their friends.

This time, before the game started one of the bigger boys, named Carl, yelled "Keepers!" which I had never heard before. I wondered what the word meant, but I naively thought it was just a twist on the rules. The game ended and I was expecting the return of my cherished beauties. This didn't happen so I asked, "When do I get my marbles back?".

Carl responded, "Are you stupid? I called keepers and that means they belong to me now."

"You mean forever?" I asked.

"Yes forever, dummy!" he snapped, mockingly.

I was surprised by this, but not terribly upset since I realized I should have asked before the game started. I really did feel stupid for not knowing that I could lose them permanently. I didn't protest and decided to accept my losses. I opened the bag and surveyed the damage. I had lost several of my favorites including two of the cat-eyes.

To make matters worse, they had been cheating severely by getting too close when they shot. Each of them had been using a "steely" which was a large heavy ball bearing. I now understood why I had been included in the game. They simply wanted to take my marbles away from me. I also understood why they had such large bags of marbles with them. They had stolen them from other kids as well.

What they lacked in sportsmanship, they made up for in ruthlessness. I knew that if I continued to play, I'd lose the remainder of my little gems. After cinching my bag, I said, "OK, thanks guys, but I don't want to play anymore." and turned away to leave.

As I started walking away, Carl's voice boomed from behind me, "Hay! Where do you think you're going sissy?"

Just then, Carl plowed into my back with a running tackle. The impact whipped my head back and knocked the wind out of me. He took me down hard with my face plowing into the gravel. As I rolled to my left side in an attempt to stand up, he began kicking my stomach. I dropped my marbles and covered my middle with my hands. He then picked them up, opened the bag and poured my collection onto the gravel. Another boy tried to kick me in the face, so I quickly brought my arm up to protect my eyes and mouth.

I stumbled to my feet, only to see the rest of my marbles being claimed by the brutal pack. As I turned to head back to the school doors, one of the teachers, acting as playground monitor, was already standing in front of me.

"What's going on?", She bellowed.

One of the boys blurted out "Nothing, miss Standish."

I looked at her and said sadly, "They stole my marbles."

"Come on boys, give them back." She demanded.

The bullies sheepishly looked through their sizable bags of ill-gotten loot. They handed me a few well worn, and frosted pieces of glass that were badly chipped. I looked at the garbage they handed me and said, "those aren't mine.", I dropped them and walked away. Just then the bell rang and I knew I could go back inside.

I sat in the classroom with my face and stomach hurting. My ears were ringing from the beating and from the chilled wind on the playground. Nothing else bad happened that day, but what had already occurred was bad enough. Every time I remembered my cherished marbles, I thought I might cry. It wasn't because they were gone, but the way they had been taken from me that made me so sad.

Adding to my sadness was the fact that they were a birthday present from Papa. He had smiled with great satisfaction when he saw excitement on my face. He had even taken time to show me how to "shoot" my marbles. I knew it made him happy to know that I was thrilled by the gift. "What will I say if he asks about them?", I thought, choking back tears.

I was beginning to understand that it was going to be a long year. When I returned home that afternoon, my mother noticed the speckled marks on my face cause by the gravel and asked about them. Once again, I twisted the truth with "Oh, I fell during recess." She surveyed the damage, shook her head and sent me outside to play.

The cold wind of autumn had died down. Even though it was fall, it was one of the last remaining days of pleasant weather before the snow and cold claimed the mountains. There were no other children out that afternoon which was usually the case. I sat on a large dirt hill overlooking the drainage ditch that ran along the road north of the lot. I noticed the culvert and felt it was time to pray once more.

I was warned to stay away from the culvert by my parents. They had explained the extreme danger it posed for a young child if a sudden cloud burst happened. Flashfloods were fairly common in Leadville, but mostly in spring and summer. I looked at the sky and didn't see many clouds, so I thought it was safe. After all, it was the only place I could pray without being heard. I always made sure that I wasn't seen entering or exiting the dark, forbidden realm.

I knew that the problem with my life was me, but I didn't know how to change what I was. And so, I thought maybe this time God will hear me and fix what was broken inside. Even though there was some concern about the danger, I made up my mind to brave the twilight under the road.

It was a large culvert, about three feet high and very long. In order to enter, I had to get on my hands and knees. I proceeded to crawl along until the circles of daylight on either side were about the same size. This indicated I had arrived at the center and reduced the chance that I'd be overheard.

The culvert was just tall enough to permit a kneeling position as long as I kept my head bowed. That made it the perfect place for a young child to pray. The moist, dank darkness became my secret church on many occasions. Sometimes an animal carcass washed into the sanctuary fouling the air for weeks. On this day, however, the tunnel was clean and the sand left on the bottom made it easier to crawl.

This place of solitude always sounded funny to me. The noise of cars passing over the road, and other background noise, like dogs barking outside the corrugated metal tube, took on a metallic echoing quality. I wasn't the only one who noticed the strange echo. Other kids would use large rocks to smack the top of the metal that extended from the ground. They did this to hear the strange sound bouncing eerily off of the grey metal walls. The bizarre, other worldly sounds made that place feel like the loneliest place on earth, but I was just fine with that. To me, it felt safe to be alone.

I began with, "God, it's me, Jody. I know you're mad at me and may even hate me, but please help me." I took a long breath and said, "I know it must have been something I did that made me this way, but I'm so sorry. If you can tell me what it was, I'll try to fix it. I want to be a boy because I know that's how you made me, but I don't know how."

I paused, looking in both directions to make sure there were no distant listeners. Seeing only the round circles of daylight, I knew that God and no one else would hear my desperate plea for help.

I continued, "Well, I guess if I'm honest, I don't really want to be a boy, but I want to be what you want me to be. I want to make you happy." I thought for a moment and said "I don't know how to want what I don't want, but I'm asking you to help me want something different." then added, "If that makes sense." Once again, I stopped to think.

"I'm just so confused, Lord!" I blurted out, as I began to cry.

"Please God, please. I know it's my fault, but I don't know what to do!", I wined, as I began to sob. My face was wet from snot and tears and I noticed that I was starting to sweat and my clothes were getting moist from the effort.

I poured out my soul without pretense before my Lord. In the dark, cold tunnel my voice began to falter as the desperate sobs overtook my breathing. "Please, please, please." I droned on in gut-wrenching squeals.

"I don't even know what to ask for except to be fixed." I sobbed. I had to drop to my hands and knees again because my body was starting to shake. In a long guttural grown I forced out the words. "God, please." Once more.

I remained on my hands and knees for quite some time, searching for words that God would listen to. I didn't know how to bargain with God or even if he was listening. Occasionally, I'd whimper, "Please God!". "Tell me what to do.".

This went on until I realized there was nothing left to say or ask. As the tears subsided, I felt better having tried, even if the response was silence once again. "Well, I guess I'm done now." I quietly said. And closed with, "Thank you for hearing my prayer, Amen."

In truth, I had no way of knowing if God had heard my prayer at all. I sometimes wondered if there really was a God. But mostly, I figured that God ignored me because he just didn't like me. Why should he like me? No one else did. Well, my family loved me, but that's just because they didn't know who I really was.

I sat in the tunnel wondering if I had anything else to say. I wondered if there was anything, I could offer that would convince God that I deserved to be fixed. But in truth, I didn't feel like I deserved anything but punishment, especially from God. Still, I hoped that I could find the words that would finally change God's mind about me. I wanted so badly to have him find something in me that was worth saving. After a few minutes of thought and despair, I got back on my hands and knees and began to crawl out of the dark, cold echoing tube.

As I was crawling toward the light, I heard my mother calling me for dinner. I tried to hurry but that was difficult in the cramped culvert and the attempt to crawl faster only soiled my clothes more. When I emerged, I tried to brush off the dirt, but my sweaty clothes made that impossible.

I returned to my home knowing that the filthy state of my shirt and jeans would raise suspicion. Entering the culvert was the kind of thing that would result in a spanking. So, I prepared a believable story about why I was so filthy. Surprisingly, my parents accepted the story and I went to clean up for dinner.

Entering the little tunnel was a common event for me. I sometimes prayed or cried, but often I would just sit in the middle far away from the outside world that wanted to hurt me. It remained my private refuge for all the years we lived in that apartment.

Several weeks into the school year, I returned home after an especially brutal day and sat on the bed. I was playing with an electrical cord that had been left after my dad replaced a lamp plug. It was tan and about two feet long.

I'm not sure where the idea came from, but I used the cord to punish myself. I rolled it up and stuffed it into my pocket as I headed to the bathroom. I pulled my pants down but left my underwear in place as I sat on the toilet. I removed the cord and straitened it. I sat there feeling the heavy plastic in my hands.

I repeated the words, "What are you looking at, fairy!". This was followed by a swishing sound and a loud crack as I unleashed the cord against my bare legs. The pain made me gasp as I stifled a scream and doubled over. A bright red welt appeared on my milky skin. I used my fingers to feel the raised stripe that I had created. Just touching it brought fiery waves of pain.

Again, I raised the makeshift whip and said, "Don't stand next to me, homo!" as I brought it down against my tender legs. Again, and again, I repeated the terrible words that others had thrown my way. Every time I brought the instrument of self-harm down on my exposed thighs, I felt a sick satisfaction for punishing the person that had made my life hell. That person was me, and I punished myself for being different.

After several minutes I could see a crisscross pattern through watery eyes. In a few places I had struck myself too hard and blood blisters were noticeable beneath the surface. I pulled up my pants, put the cord back in my pocket and left the bathroom with my legs burning.

I blamed myself for my suffering. After all, there was nobody else to blame. There had been a number of cruel adults, dozens of bullies and all of my classmates. They had all taught me that I was worthless. None who understood what I was, had ever shown me mercy. Even God had no sympathy for me. I knew that I was the problem, and I hated myself for it. Of all the abusers I faced, the one who turned out to be the worst, was me.

The school year progressed, but the ridicule, name calling and physical violence persisted. At times, I felt myself shutting down emotionally. Sometimes I felt like a robot walking through my life not caring about anything. Other times I cared way too much but could do nothing to change what was happening to me. It all felt so hopeless.

I Can Fly

WHEN YOU FINALLY come to believe that everything you are and all that you hope for, is not simply inadequate, but truly evil, you lose yourself to the desire for oblivion. As a young child I had on many occasions imagined changing into a bird and flying away from all the pain and the people who hated me. One day as I gazed out of the school window, "Flying" took on another meaning. "I could jump off of something high.", I whispered to myself.

The thought embedded its self in my still developing brain. It was a solution I had not considered before. I began to imagine myself plummeting to the ground. I imagined "flying" to freedom and release. In that classroom of suffering, an eight-year-old began a plan to leave this world.

It was at this time I also tried desperately to change. I truly didn't understand how people knew what was wrong with me. I never once said that I was a girl. I had never said that to anyone. I never said anything that could be considered female, or so I thought. But they knew, they all knew. Somehow, everyone but my parents knew perfectly well what I was.

Years after this, I began to understand that it was the way I walked, and talked and held my books, and laughed and a hundred other things that gave me away. I didn't have to say a word to broadcast to the world what was going on inside.

I didn't know how everyone knew, but I thought that if I could rid myself of the desire to be a girl, things would be all right. Every time I began thinking of being a girl, I quickly interrupted the thought with, "Stop it! That's stupid and wrong! Do you want God to stay mad at you? Idiot!" Sometimes my self-talk was more positive. Like, "Hey, stop that. You want your life to get better, don't you?" or "This is not going to make you happy." "I know I can be a boy if I really try."

Even though I was trying to change myself, I found myself frequently considering death as the best option. Oddly enough, there was no sadness when I fantasized about dying. In fact, I felt something I hadn't felt for a long time. I felt at peace whenever I thought about ending my life. Of course, there was the idea of what happens after my life is over.

I don't remember how I discovered the next terrible truth about God, but it made me feel even more trapped and desperate. I learned that killing myself was a sin. In fact, I was told it was the worst sin I could commit. It was the only "unforgivable" sin. The logic was that we can ask to be forgiven for anything, even murder, as long as we truly regret it and turn away from it. But, if we murder ourselves, we can't ask for forgiveness and turn away from the sin. And so, I thought that suicide would buy me a direct ticket to Hell. This was a terrible realization. How can I rid myself of the life that I found unbearable without launching myself into a world that was even worse?

One night, I was in my bed awake and issuing whispered prayers. "I know I don't deserve heaven, but can you please not send me to Hell, Lord?" Such questions, and indeed all of my prayers were met with silence. "I know you don't like what I am, but at least I've never tried to hurt anyone." I paused for a moment and continued with, "Well, except for myself. I have tried to hurt myself, but only me. And you agree that I should be hurt, right?" I paused again before continuing my request. "I don't even tell lies, like the other kids." I stopped and added, "much." Because I knew I was hiding the truth from everyone which was just as dishonest as telling lies. I even fibbed to my parents to cover up beatings.

I continued, "Since I won't be able to go to heaven, and I don't want to go to Hell, can you just make me, gone?", I begged. "You know, like you use a gigantic eraser and make me, just go away? Please?" I explained, "Just make me disappear like I never existed at all. Then, you don't have to punish me, but you can still get rid of me." Then I added, "You'll never get sick looking at me again." It was like I was asking God for permission to do what I was considering. Since he didn't object, I took that as a yes. But in truth, I was still a little worried I'd end up burning forever.

Eventually, I resolved to go to the top floor of the apartment building and jump from the fire escape. I knew I'd have to wait until the stormy weather had improved, but at least there was a possible plan to finally get rid of the sorrow, loneliness, shame, and guilt. There was finally a path to take that would end my miserable life. Since I now understood that the problem was me, I was determined to get rid of the problem. Sometimes when I thought about it, I'd whisper, "No more Jody." to myself when I was alone.

Once the storm system had died down, I was permitted to go outside to play. It wasn't a warm day at all, but nice days wouldn't come for at least another month or two. We had been cooped up for so long that mom let me go out, but kept my sister inside. Mom, made me put on a slippery snow suit, oversized mittens and a scarf and a knit hat. In those days, we wore regular shoes inside of rubber boots called galoshes. Nothing I wore, was designed to give stability or traction on snow and ice. I wondered if I could even get to the top floor before sliding off.

I didn't intend to end my life that day, I just wanted to see if I could sneak up to the top floor. I needed to check out the fire escapes. This was just a scouting trip, or so I thought. I chose a fire escape as far from my family's apartment as I could because I didn't want to be spotted. Then I started climbing up the half rotted, wooden construction. It was slow going.

Not only were my small legs barely up to the challenge of climbing the stairs with so many icy spots, but my mittens made holding on to the railing near my head almost impossible. So, I removed my mittens and used my bare hands to hold on. This worked for a while, but my fingers got numb quickly and began to lose what little strength my tiny fingers had.

By the time I reached the top of the stairs and the final platform, my hands were like ice and my nose was running. I looked at the wooden deck in front of me which had begun to sag and slope a little towards rotted and broken rails. In fact, there was a gap where the lower rail was missing all together. This left a wide, menacing opening directly in front of me with only two rails. The top one was about as high as my head and another about chest high. I paused for a long time as the cold wind hissed by. I cautiously stepped on to the deck which was covered in frozen dog pee.

As soon as I stepped fully on to the ice, my rubber boots slipped out from underneath me. My numb fingers were not able to hold on, as I went down with a thud that knocked the breath out of me. To my horror, I found I was still moving. I was sliding toward the gap! Then I stopped for a moment as my galoshes snagged something. It was a nail sticking up only slightly, but it was enough for the rubber on the boot to grab hold. When I stopped sliding, I sat there trying not to move.

I was half sitting and half reclining on my forearms. I could smell the dog urine under my elbows and butt. It was then that I heard the distant voice of my mother, calling me. "Jody? Jody?" When I heard her, I thought about how heartbroken she was going to be. I imagined her and my dad crying. Only then did I understand the kind of suffering I'd bring into their lives. It was enough to make me stop wanting to die.

I realized how selfish I was being and decided not to kill myself. Unfortunately, it could have been too late. I was in a dangerous situation, and death loomed only a few feet away. All I could think about was getting home and getting warm.

I looked behind me at the vertical post which represented safety. I rolled over slightly and reached for the post. I strained to grab the rough wood that had been painted several times. The old paint was slippery and I found it too difficult. My tiny hands were turning blue and completely numb so I couldn't close tight enough to grab hold.

As I was desperately trying to grip the post, it slipped out of my hand and began to get farther away. I rolled over on my belly in order to reach it. I was beginning to slide sideways on my stomach! I could see the unprotected edge of the fire escape, and to my horror, started to spin as I slid. Now, I was sliding head first toward the menacing gap. "This is it." I thought, "Soon I'll be flying." It wasn't supposed to happen today.", I thought, as tears began to stream from my eyes.

As my head neared the edge, the snow suit under my stomach snagged a large wooden knot and I stopped. I was still looking at the paved alley below. I didn't dare move for fear that I'd start sliding again, and even a few inches more could mean death. I saw how far down I would fall, and regretted being head first. As I laid there terrified with my heart pounding, I heard my mother still calling from the distance and wanted to see her so badly. "She'll never see me alive again." I realized.

As I laid there staring at my fate far below, I heard the unmistakable sound of the kitchen door open behind me. A man's voice boomed, "What the hell you doing up here kid?" "Ya wanna die?" Then I felt a single strong hand grab the back of my snowsuit like he was crumpling a tissue. He lifted me to my feet and I was able to see a very angry and terrified bald man looking me straight in the eyes. He pushed me toward the stairs as I slipped and landed on my butt once again.

"Sorry Sir!", I shouted through snot and tearing eyes.

"Get out of here kid! I don't ever want to see you up here again!", He barked.

"Yes Sir. I'm sorry Sir!", I answered.

I half slid and half fell down the flight of stairs in an attempt to make it all go away. As I reached the bottom of the top flight, I turned to see a still angry man shaking his head and demanding to know who my parents were.

"Sorry Sir" I kept repeating, "You won't see me again Sir."

As I reached the ground, the man was still watching me and yelling "What's your name kid?"

I didn't answer and just kept running. A more distant but still angry voice, sounded, "Stupid kid!"

I was trying to put distance between myself and the very upset man, but unfortunately, I was headed away from my apartment as well. I think the reason he didn't pursue me was because he had been sleeping. Many times, mine workers slept during the days when they had been assigned the night shift, which everyone called graveyard. I knew this because my grandfather often worked graveyard shifts as well.

I rounded the corner of the building where I was out of his sight and began working my way back to my mother's now desperate sounding voice. I kept trying to wipe the tears and snot off of my face to conceal the evidence of my stupidity. I had to make sure the man didn't follow me home and tell my mom what had happened.

When I got back, I came up the front stairwell so she wouldn't know where I had been. When I came in the front door, my mother practically screaming, said, "Where were you?" "I almost called the police!"

She continued to scold me, but I was so relieved to be home that I didn't mind. She eventually calmed down and helped me undress and blow my nose. I almost panicked when I remembered the dog pee and was afraid that she'd notice the smell. I think it was the rich aroma of the soup on the stove that covered the smell of the urine. It wafted through the house and made my belly churn with anticipation. I went to the bathroom and washed off the leftover slime and removed the snowsuit.

Then I joined her and my sister and had hot chicken noodle soup at the kitchen table. My sister sat there with wide eyes and an expression that told me she didn't understand the volume of my mother's voice. I smiled at her but she just frowned and said, "Mommy's mad at you." I knew she didn't like the fact that I had done something to cause my mom to raise her voice. They were both a bit angry, but eating the simple canned soup with both of them was wonderful, and warmed more than my body.

Over the next few weeks, I replayed the event in my mind many times and realized how stupid I was to even go up there. Afterwards, I always avoided that section of the apartment complex and the man who had saved my life. Unfortunately, I continued to entertain thoughts of "flying to freedom" for years to come.

Music of Hope

DURING THESE DAYS of torture that felt unending, there were occasional forays into the land of joy. These were bright spots in an otherwise dark grey and black painting. There were the classes that took us away from our normal classroom and away from the hurt that had become habitual actions for my tormentors. Physical Education was not much better. It's amazing how inventive kids can be in order to inflict pain on the weaker boys. However, music class was another story.

Music was a beam of sunlight in my dungeon of despair. In music class, we sometimes played rudimentary percussion instruments, but mostly we sang. I loved singing and tried really hard to be good at it. It was one of the few things that I put real effort into. Music got me away from my home room and let me meet with kids who didn't know me, or about me. This was especially true with choir which included all of the students in third and fourth grade.

As fate would have it, a school play was scheduled in the latter part of the year. I don't remember the subject of the play, just that is involved a nature theme. It was most likely something to do with the approaching spring.

The winters in Leadville were particularly long and hard. In fact, our town sat in a valley with an elevation of more than ten thousand feet above sea level. Denver, "The Mile-high City" had at least two more months of nice weather than we experienced. Snow gripped the town from October to May. Consequently, the very idea of spring lifted the spirits of students, teachers and parents alike.

When the students received their assignments for the play, most of the boys were given rolls as lions or trees or even rocks. Two of the smaller "boys" with the prettiest voices joined the girls as singing birds and one of them was me. This thrilled me for a lot of reasons. I liked the fact that I was being included with the girls, but mostly I loved the idea of being a bird. I would often imagine being a bird so that I could fly away from those who so often wanted to hurt me.

The costumes that were given the "birds" seemed distinctly feminine with long multi-colored crape paper feathers trailing from our arms like wings. We also had similar feathers attached to the back of our pants to simulate tails. I pretended that my "tail" was a skirt. We were given small "beaks" made of construction paper which opened and closed as we sang. I absolutely adored the blue and pink costume that was given to me, but it was a mixed blessing. It solicited mocking comments from some of the students, but the teasing and bulling that constantly shaded my world couldn't have been worse. So, I shrugged it off as best as I could and focused on the delight of being a bird with the other girls.

Every time we went to rehearse for the play, I got excited that I could pretend to be a bird again. The fact that they included me with the girls could have been seen as another attempt to humiliate me and perhaps it was. But I never detected even the slightest disgust on the part of the play organizers. In fact, I wondered if they knew about me and included me with the girls as a kindness. I even imagined that I could be myself and tell the truth and that I might be accepted by some. The idea of letting the world know who I truly was and being accepted in spite of that reality was tempting. But in the end, it was just a fantasy that I never acted upon.

Eventually, the play was performed which ended the rehearsals, the costume and this wonderful episode of my young life. My vacation from sadness was over, but I still cherish the memories of hope that it inspired.

There were other outings that occurred before the end of the year that I enjoyed very much. Any trip that got me away from the school and out of that crucible of sorrow was enthusiastically welcomed. We were allowed to go on two fieldtrips to sing and hear the local choirs sing at other schools, but the best outing of all happened just before the school year ended.

One beautiful spring day, we were told that we'd be attending a play at the local high school. They always used the younger children for practice in live rehearsals before presenting the play to the rest of the town. The teachers rounded us up in preparation of the walk across town and up the hill to the auditorium. We had to cross several roads so there was an ample number of teachers on hand to ensure our safety. So, I wasn't too worried about bullies and the walk turned out to be quite enjoyable.

When we entered the school and the auditorium where the play was performed, I was awestruck. We had nothing similar in the elementary school and the size and grandeur of the location, made an immediate impact. The plays I had experienced before that day were performed on a small stage in the gymnasium. But this place had obviously been built for just such a purpose. Looking back, it's amusing just how easily I was impressed with the simple grandeur our high school could pull off.

The play was The Sound of Music and since I loved singing, and the main character was female, it was perfect. I immediately identified with the primary heroine, Maria. The young lady who elegantly portrayed her had a beautiful voice and presence. But it was the storyline and the character of Maria that instantly captured my imagination.

She was a young woman who didn't behave the way her peers and superiors wanted. For a time, I was afraid for Maria. I feared that she might end up being hurt as I had been. But as the story turned from one of unfair judgment to one of triumph, I began to feel hope. That hope was not just for Maria, but also for myself. The singing and sets were very well done and I sat there mesmerized by the spectacle. It turned out to be one of the most impactful, and beautiful memories of the school year. Years later, I was able to watch the movie starring Julie Andrews and felt many of the same emotions I felt on that wonderful spring day. I felt the joyful expectation that perhaps, my life too would get better.

Summers were always glorious in Leadville. It never got too hot, and the dry smell of the dense pine forests was carried on every breath of wind hissing through the treetops. The sharp chirps of squirrels were everywhere and the song birds contributed their voices to the sweet sounds of a mountain summer. These and other delicious summer sensations were already with us during recess and after school. Thunderstorms had replaced the snow and bitter cold.

I knew it wouldn't be long before school ended and I was once again free from the people who caused me so much sorrow. As the school year drew to a close, the play was still fresh in my mind. Ending the school year on such a positive note of hope, made the start of summer even more glorious. A child could almost imagine that life was a good thing and not to be ended as I so often desired.

Before long I found myself on the first day of summer vacation. It felt like heaven and the beauty of life returned and my injured heart was allowed to heal once more, at least for a time. Summers at that age felt like they would last forever and I could completely release the fear that gripped me for nine months of the year.

One beautiful summer day, my grandparents showed up with three of my cousins and we all loaded into my grandfather's large Plymouth station wagon. We all called him Papa. Well, everyone but my grandmother. They referred to each other as Ma and Pa, which didn't seem comical at the time, but now brings a smile to my face when I think about how "Back woods" it sounded. They were from Alabama which was also where my mother was born and spent her childhood. Most recently they had lived in Wyoming while Papa worked at the coal mines there.

I always enjoyed the days when I got to hang out with my cousins. Even though I knew they weren't actually my friends, they tolerated me when my family was around. However, when they were with real friends, they usually shunned me. My cousin's friends weren't invited on family outings, so they could afford kindness without paying for it socially. We lived in different parts of the town and attended different schools, so they didn't know the full extent of my awkwardness or my loneliness. The family I had in Leadville spent quite a bit of time together and so, there were days I got to pretend I was just a normal kid.

That day we went for a long drive and some hiking near Turquoise Lake. We often visited this area because it was so close to town. The rich scenery and number of activities possible there always made it an adventure.

It was one of the places my family liked to fish. There were cabins along the shoreline on the south. When we fished there, it was usually on the north side. The rustic docks and cabins across the water looked like a painting or postcard.

Sometimes we filled sandbags in an area they called the sand pits. Other times we filled bags with black topsoil for Papa's garden. There was an abandoned turquoise mine above the lake and some days we would walk around the land outside of the mine border and pick up the small blue rocks that littered the ground there.

On this particular day We wondered through the thick pine forests and poked at the large Bolete mushrooms that grew everywhere. I watched with wide-eyed excitement as chipmunks, pine squirrels and rabbits fled from our meanderings. We took the car up to Carlton Tunnel, an old abandoned train tunnel that stretched under the Continental Divide.

On the drive up to the tunnel, I was amazed by the number of large Snowshoe Hares we saw. Within a distance of only two or three miles I counted nearly thirty of these big, fast "rabbits". They had already lost the pure white coat they wore in winter and had adopted the mottled grey, tan and brown that helped them hide during the summer months.

We were approaching timberline and it seemed that everywhere we stopped the air was thick with the smell of the high-altitude wildflowers. Water, in the form of pools and brooks surrounded us. There were springs that playfully emerged from rock faces as small waterfalls. The streams and brooks trickling under and over the road created a kind of music. Their combined voices sounded more like rain or windchimes than flowing streams. Lonely hawks could be heard screeching high above us as they soared over the thawing tundra and snow.

At one point I found myself walking with Papa on the same road but we were a few hundred feet from the others. We heard a loud noise coming from the trees above the road. As we turned to see what was happening, Papa pulled me close to protect me. A large, startled deer emerged only a few feet above us. It was in a full run and instead of dodging us, it jumped. Papa had to duck to keep the deer from running into his head. I watched in wonder as the magnificent animal passed directly over us. We watched the deer vanish on the other side of the road below us and continue through the trees. Papa looked at me to offer reassurance, but when he saw my wide-eyed amazement and huge smile, we both broke into laughter. Papa and I shared many amazing moments like that, and even though he could be scary at times, I never doubted his love.

He once told my mother, "You know, I love all of my grandchildren, but there is something special about Jody." He was always more protective of me than he was my cousins who lived with him at the time. Perhaps he sensed my vulnerability or the fact that I had been so wounded. I often wondered what he would think of me if he knew my secret. But looking back now, I wonder if he may have figured it out, but loved me anyway.

                                          TEARS IN SILENCE

There were many magical moments with my parents, grandparents and cousins that summer. There were times we spent fishing or just kicking around in the majesty of the Colorado Rockies. I'm so grateful that my young life which had such darkness, also contained supplies of extraordinary beauty and deep joy.

✺

Josephine

Summer passed too quickly as summers tend to do. For me, as the beginning of school approached, my feelings of dread grew as though I was being stalked by a menacing creature from the shadows.

I always tried to find hope, imagining that maybe this year would be the year that I made friends. I hoped that somehow, I would be accepted into some segment of society and end my unbearable loneliness. This was not going to be that year. What I didn't know at the time was that the schoolyear looming before me would turn out to be the worst year of my life and far worse than anything I could have imagined.

When the first day of class arrived, I had convinced myself that this time, I'd have friends and life would be wonderful. I sat hopefully, waiting to respond when my name was called out. For some reason, they always read the boys names first and in alphabetical order. When it dawned on me that she had already passed the "Ds" I realized I had been placed on the girl's roster once more. So, the first setback happened, but was only a slight embarrassment. The other students began to giggle when I said, "Here.", after my name was read.

It was easily remedied by moving my name to the boys list. I couldn't have realized as the schoolyear began that "my name" would become the focal point of the abusive year about to unfold. In fact, this year, it would be my teacher who would turn out to be my greatest abuser. Children can be cruel, but it takes an adult with evil intent to truly break a child, and I was about to be so utterly broken.

After only a few days of observing me, Mrs. Kelly realized who and what she was dealing with. I still have no idea why she made it her mission to destroy me. Maybe she had an issue with my parents. Or perhaps she thought she was doing me a favor by toughening me up. In any case, whatever her motivation was, the injury she inflicted and encouraged others to inflict would color my world for many years to come.

She began by making me wear a "dunce cap" while seated in the front corner of the classroom. I sat there as a spectacle and an object of ridicule. Mrs. Kelly would hurl repeated insults which only encouraged the laughter and taunting of the other students. Spit wads and rubber bands flew every time I was seated there.

It was a strange thing looking back because I was always one of the brightest students in any class. The "dunce" label was not at all appropriate for an intelligent and compliant child. It was intended for those students who showed unusually stupid or rebellious behavior. What I was, might have been despicable or horrible to some, but I was definitely not stupid. Sitting there I realized my hopes that this year things would be better, vanished as I sank deeper and deeper into despair and loneliness.

During the early part of the year, I tried my best to please Mrs. Kelly by doing my school work the way she requested, but she kept changing the rules on me. She did things like telling me to use a pencil but then grading me off for not using pen. Still, I tried to accommodate her ever changing demands. I noticed that she didn't do that to all of her students, just me and a handful of others that she deliberately sabotaged.

The saddest part was that I loved schoolwork. I was good at it, and it gave me an excuse to keep my head down and avoid eye contact. But I knew my grades were slipping because I never understood what I was supposed to be doing. To make matters worse, I was too shy to ask questions and she was never good at explaining things anyway. I eventually gave up on the schoolwork and started daydreaming a lot.

A few days after Halloween, Mrs. Kelly let us eat one of our pieces of candy before recess. I naturally chose the most attractive and large sucker in my bag. It was large enough that I was still sucking on it when the recess bell rang. So, I twisted off the soggy stick and kept it in my mouth on the way outside.

I was toward the back of the line, and as we approached the double doors leading outside, someone shoved me hard on the back. This caused me to inhale sharply, lodging the sucker in my windpipe. I tried to cough it out or swallow it down, but there was no use. I couldn't breathe at all.

The teachers on the playground were still a long distance from me, and I didn't want to make a spectacle in front of the other kids. So, I turned around to find a teacher to help me. I hoped to find one of the teachers still in her classroom or in the hall, but they were all long gone, headed to the teachers' lounge for a smoke or cup of coffee.

It was only when I found myself in an empty hall that I knew I was in trouble. I was getting dizzy from suffocation and dropped to my knees. My heart was making drumming sounds in my ears mixed with squishing noises from the blood surging into my brain. I remember seeing a little girl with red curls and with a horrified look on her face. I tried to say the words, "get help." But not even a squeak came out. My airway was completely blocked and I knew I'd die soon, as I blacked out.

The strange thing was, I knew the next thing I'd see would be God. A warm and happy sensation came over me as I surrendered my short life and hoped God would be kind. This time, I didn't have to worry about the consequences of killing myself, because it had truly been an accident. It comforted me to know I had not committed the

                                             TEARS IN SILENCE

"Unforgivable sin". I awoke a few minutes later with the left side of my face on the cold tile in a pool of vomit.

Evidently, I had thrown up with such force that it had dislodged the sucker which was also on the floor surrounded by half-digested Fruit Loops from breakfast. I didn't remember throwing up, so it must have been involuntary after everything went dark.

As I struggled to get back up, I saw the little girl who had returned with a teacher quickly walking my way to offer assistance. "Are you OK?", she panted with concern.

I answered with a croak, "I think so."

She could see the crisis had passed and said, "Go clean yourself up in the bathroom."

I looked at the mess on the floor and whispered, "I'm sorry."

"It's OK dear. I'll get a janitor. Are you sure you're, OK?" she said softly.

I took my first deep breath and answered, "Yes ma'am." Then I stood and headed to the restroom.

I stood at the sink and washed the vomit off of my face. I checked in the mirror to make sure it was all gone. I stared at the now clean face and whispered "I hate you!" Once more I uttered the words, but this time louder. My voice echoed off the walls of the empty restroom. "I hate you! I wish you had died!" I barked at the sad child in the mirror. I felt cheated. I finally had a way to die that wouldn't land me in hell, but it had been stollen from me. I took a deep breath and walked out.

When I returned from the restroom, the janitor was almost done with the mess, and I stopped to offer my apology once more. I returned to my life like nothing had happened. But I remembered the sense of peace that day. It was something I knew I had to hide from my parents. It wouldn't be good if they knew I wanted to die.

Weeks passed and the abuse continued for what felt like years. Every afternoon after school I sat in my bedroom exhausted and on the verge of tears. I was breaking inside, and with each passing day it became more unbearable. I longed for some escape but nothing presented itself except death, and that was beyond consideration, well, almost.

I began to cheer up when the holidays approached. Christmas break was close and my spirits were always better before Christmas. It was always such a wonderful time for me. There were the decorations which I loved. And of course, the holidays brought with it pumpkin pies and cookies. The smell of the apartment and my grandmother's house was enough to lift anyone's spirits. I got to spend those days with family which was my only source of social connection. But the most important thing was that I could get away from school and the bullying for a few weeks.

It was such an important thing to me at that age. A break from school meant I could be a kid for a few precious days. Christmas vacation and other smaller breaks represented some of my only hopes and something I knew would come if I could just hold on a little longer. The holidays came, but were gone too soon. It was time to go back and endure everything once again.

A few weeks after Christmas break, Mrs. Kelly called for the attention of the classroom and made me stand up in front of everyone. She then announced that she was going to change my name. She explained that "Jody" was not nearly girly enough for me and explained that the students would now be calling me Josephine. This of course solicited a roar of laughter and ridicule from the other students. I knew that things had just taken a turn for the worst.

As I took my seat, one of the girls sitting near me began with "Josephine, Josephine, you're really a girl aren't you, Josephine?" The sing-song ridicule was true, but I could never admit that to anyone. I really was a girl, and wanted to shout it out loud, but never did.

Mrs. Kelly followed through with her threat by making sure my actual name only appeared on official rosters and documents that my parents saw. All others, such as signup sheets and seating charts bore the "Name of Shame." The other kids were not only encouraged to call me by this name, but students who called me Jody were reprimanded or even punished.

I tried to bear my humiliation with as much grace and dignity as I could, but in the end, it began to destroy me. I quit doing the worksheets or any class assignments. I quit talking to anyone at school unless it was absolutely necessary, and retreated into a world of daydreams and fantasy. I completely disconnected from the world in which I found myself imprisoned. The only time I came out of hiding was when the three o'clock bell rang and I knew once more I'd see my family and be on my way home.

I always tried to be the last child to exit and reenter the class room. I found that having other students behind me presented the greatest risk, but this was the year that changed. One day, as we left the classroom, I felt a sharp stinging sensation on my left butt cheek that almost made me scream. I'd been stung by bees, but this was far worse. As I turned to see what had bitten me, I saw Mrs. Kelly holding a three-inch hat pin that she had stabbed me with. She wore a broad and sinister smile as she tucked the pin in her pocket. From then on, I tried hard to keep myself from ever getting too close to that awful woman again. Unfortunately, it wouldn't be the last time the hat pin was used.

The school year continued and I tried not to think about the fact that I was getting all failing grades. Eventually, I'd have to face my parents and explain. Unfortunately, I was about to learn that there was a far more terrifying consequence to not doing my schoolwork.

It was in the midst of this darkness and despair that a very peculiar thing occurred. One evening my parents let us stay up late and watch "Rowan & Martin's Laugh-in". To be honest, I didn't understand most of the "adult" jokes which was probably why dad permitted us to stay up and watch. There were silly voices and skits with costumes. But this night, A joke would sink straight through to my very soul.

I don't remember who was involved in the joke, or the names they used for the characters, but I remember what it meant. It went something like this.

"Did you hear about Bob?"

"No, what about him?

"He had to go to Sweden for an operation."

"Oh dear, how did it turn out?"

"Oh, she's just fine now."

My face began to warm as I blushed, certain that everyone in the room would know about my terrible secret. My heart began to pound as I tried to control my breathing. I thought, "No way." "I must be misunderstanding it." My father seated behind me, was laughing. So, as calmly and as casually as I could, I turned around and asked, "What did that joke mean?" To my shock and utter disbelief, he answered, "Oh, he just went off and had a sex change."

I turned back around and tried hard to control my emotions and my face. But this was the most Earthshattering revelation I had experienced since that day I found out that I was a boy.

Two amazing truths emerged from this event. The first changed my view of who I was forever. "There are others like me?" I thought. I had always assumed I was uniquely cursed. I thought that I was a fluke of nature, and it was my issue and only mine. But now, I understood that there were others who felt the same way. The second revelation was the term "Sex change". "Oh my", I thought. There is something that can be done about this problem.

I went to bed that night still in a state of shock and wonder over that simple joke. Yes, it was a joke, which made it obvious that people who had a "Sex change" were ridiculous. But for the first time in my life, it was "people", and not just me. The internet didn't exist in 1968. To search for such information at the county library was unthinkable, especially in a small town where everyone knows your business. Still, a small ember of hope had been kindled within me and the term "sex change" would forever be an idea that would serve as a lifeline on many occasions.

As the idea meandered through my ten-year-old head. I eventually understood that such a thing was not possible for me. The ridicule, hurt and despair that such an action would cause for my family was unthinkable. Still, I dared to dream that it was possible in a far distant future. "Yeah, maybe someday", I thought.

As the end of the school year approached, I found myself staring out the window of the classroom daydreaming about the fast-approaching summer break. This was the time of year when students begin counting down to the last day of school. To me it felt like I had served a brutal prison sentence and was anxiously awaiting my release. I couldn't help but feel joy and hope rising. Although I had to contend with the ridicule and bullying that were always the backdrop of my young life, I still felt a measure of cheer. I knew that much of my suffering would soon end, at least for a few months.

I looked out at a spring landscape where winter had finally been defeated by the longer sunny days. As I did, I became aware of a large menacing shape standing to my right and behind me. It was Mrs. Kelly. As I turned to look at her, I noticed she wore a peculiar smile that instilled dread, although I wasn't sure why.

She pulled up a chair and sat next to me. "It looks like you and I are going to get to spend a lot more time together."

As she spoke these words, my chest tightened and my pulse began to race. It felt as though my heart was working its way into my throat and would soon be vomited out of my mouth. "What do you mean?", I responded, with a broken voice almost whispering.

Gleefully she responded, "I'm keeping you back. You get to repeat the fourth grade." She studied my face in order to relish the look of panic, despair and shock. As she stood and looked back at me, it appeared as though she would break into maniacal laughter.

Resistance

Mrs. Kelly returned to her desk and sat down. She continued to observe me still wearing the ghoulish smile. I glanced around the room. I saw the faces of my tormentors and realized they would all be allowed to move on. Their lives would continue to progress and unfold. Whereas, I was destined to receive another year of heartbreak and pain. I felt there would never be an end to my nightmare.

Something happened inside me at that moment. I no longer cared about anything. I didn't care about her or the other students. I didn't care what people thought of me and I certainly didn't care about what happened to me. I folded my arms and put my head on the desk. However, I didn't know what was coming.

"Sit up straight!" came the command from the front of the classroom.

I did not comply.

"Sit up this instant!" she barked, in an angry voice.

I remained motionless. As I heard her rise and the sound of her heals thundering toward me, I almost lost my nerve. But in deliberate defiance I didn't even bother to look at the calamity headed my way. I felt an angry hand wrap itself around my wrist as Mrs. Kelly yanked me from my seat. She did this with such violence that I was thrown across the aisle striking my head against the steal leg of the nearest desk. Still, I did nothing, but sat on the floor waiting for the next blow but not really caring.

She grabbed me by the wrist once more and tried to force me to stand. She was not successful.

"That does it! You're going to the principal's office." She yelled.

She started for the door dragging me behind her. I tried to remain seated, but found that because of the angles my body was spinning and turning wildly, so I laid down. I covered my face with my other arm and stopped resisting. Once again, I felt my head hit something hard. It was the steal doorframe. Being dragged through the spring-loaded door, I felt the bottom of the door jaggedly scraping across my stomach and legs.

Once in the hall she dropped me and demanded I stand. I remained on the floor, motionless, not uttering a word or launching any retaliation. "Get up!", she demanded. I responded with silent noncompliance. Once again, she grabbed me and started dragging me down the hall.

The hallway was divided, with one section of the hall being a few feet higher than the other. In the center of the hall was a small staircase of only a few steps. "She's going to drag me down the stairs.", I thought.

There was a welded steel railing on the steps. As the stairs came rushing toward me, I decided the railing was safety and I was determined to anchor myself to it. I rolled quickly to my left and was able to wrench my wrist out of her grip. By the time she turned around to grab me again, I had latched onto the vertical support. I wrapped both arms and legs around it as tight as I could and bowed my head into my chest. I must have looked like a frightened hedgehog clinging to a sapling in that dark hallway.

She tried to pry me away from my refuge, but to no avail. She hit me hard in the back of the head, but in the end my skull proved tougher than her fist. She whispered threats in my ear.

"I'll call the police and have you arrested for truancy." she growled.

I almost gave in when she told me she was going to go call my parents. But I remained committed to the stronghold. I felt a sharp pain on my left leg when she kicked me, but I didn't budge. She stood there for a few moments in exasperation and then headed back to the classroom. She opened the door and to my surprise called to me, "Well, are you coming? Or should I call for the principal?".

I thought about it for a second or two, stood up and started walking back to the classroom. But this time, as I walked through the door, I looked her in the eyes. As I entered the room and sat down, I felt a sense of power. The other kids were looking at me in disbelief and terror. I had fought the monster and was still alive. It was a small victory, but for someone so use to constant defeat and loss, it felt pretty good.

I turned my eyes back to the wonderful spring day just beyond the glass. I smiled, because I knew something Mrs. Kelly did not. I would soon be out of her clutches and I would never see her face again.

The summer was going to be amazing and wonderful. It had to be, because there would never be another, at least not for me. I finally made a firm promise to myself that I would never again set foot in this classroom or any other classroom. Never again would I let an abusive teacher have their way with me. I was older now, almost ten, and was well practiced at planning my death. I looked at Mrs. Kelly and smiled at her still scowling face.

It felt like I was on a boat slowly sliding away from the dock and out of her reach. I was headed for a place I couldn't imagine yet, but I knew it would be nothing like Earth. I turned back to the window and took a deep and satisfying breath. "I'd have to make it look like an accident, I thought." Accidents happen, and it's always sad when a child dies, but suicide is much worse.

I didn't want my folks thinking they had failed me. In fact, the only love and kindness I had ever known on a regular basis came from my family. I knew they would be heartbroken. Still, I knew I'd never endure another school year with this monstrous woman.

I looked out the window again and imagined fishing with my dad or "Papa". Although Papa was a rough coal miner from Alabama, he was kind to me. And even though most people would not have called him a gentle soul, he always treated me with tenderness. It was like he could sense my vulnerability and perhaps even my femininity. My father, who was a bit more oblivious to my true nature, and even tougher, was fair and kind as well. I loved them both and cherished the time they spent with me. I would miss them when I was gone, and I would miss my mother too. She sang songs with my sister and I, and helped us draw or paint. She was a beautiful woman, or at least I thought so. Even the terrifying "Lizard face" that we begged her to make when she was pretending to "eat us up" would be missed.

"Yep, this will be the best summer ever." I thought. "It will be my last summer, but all the more reason to make it special.", I decided. As terrible as it sounds now, the idea of ending my young life after a long and perfect summer gave me a considerable amount of joy.

Interestingly, a few days after my decision, our class was visited by a woman I had never encountered before. I didn't know it at the time, but this woman was going to change my life and save me from both Mrs. Kelly and suicide.

The woman who visited our class was different from most of the disinterested teachers in our school, and very, very different from Mrs. Kelly. She was kind, and explained things well. She even smiled at me as if she actually liked me. I told myself it's because she doesn't know about me, but it didn't matter. Because she was kind and treated me with respect, I decided to try to do as she asked. She was there to give us all a "special" test. She said it was an "IQ" test and explained how to fill out the forms. This was different from any I had ever encountered before. We were told to indicate our answers by filling in little circles on the paper with a pencil. I had never seen forms like that before but was determine to try for her sake.

The test didn't seem particularly hard and I enjoyed the orderly rows of little circles, which always had the correct answer as one of the choices. I enjoyed the soft, slippery feel of the pencil when I darken one of the circles. I even enjoyed the smell and feel of the paper that they were printed on. Once we finished, she collected them and took them with her.

I remember hoping I'd see her again, but that didn't happen. Somewhere, in some room, they took the tests and examined them and counted up all the results and changed my fate. Eventually the results came in and Mrs. Kelly informed me herself what the IQ test had revealed. I'm not sure how many days it took to get the results back. But it turned out to be one of the last days of school, and the very best day of the entire year.

Mrs. Kelly approached me and pulled up a chair next to me. I noticed that there was something quite different about her attitude. She seemed almost apologetic with her words. She explained that I was not going to be repeating the fourth grade after all. She went on to explain that the test we had taken showed that I was "exceptionally bright" and that there was no need to make me repeat the year. I didn't quite understand." How could a simple test take her power away?", I asked myself. Then it dawned on me that her inability to teach someone who was "bright" had pointed to her as the problem rather than any failure on my part. I concealed my joy and responded with, "Hmm". Then turned my gaze back to the window as if to say, "You no longer matter."

We sat silent for a moment and then she said, "I see you looking out the window a lot. What do you think about?" I turned to meet her eyes directly and in the most adult voice I could manage, responded with, "I think about the origin of the universe and the nature of God." She was dumbfounded. Of course, that was not completely true. Most of the time I was wishing I could die or imagining her bursting into flames. Still, I relished the look of surprise and humility that spread across her face. After a long pause she lowered her eyes, stood and said, "Well, that's something people don't usually think about until they're much older." I watched as she walked slowly back to her desk. Not only had I won my freedom from this awful prison, but had disgraced my captor on the way out. It was a truly delicious experience. I sometimes feel guilty that I took such pleasure in her embarrassment, but in truth, she simply got what she deserved.

Arts and Crafts

I ENTERED MIDDLE school as a deeply traumatized child. Anytime I was away from the safety of home, I was sullen, withdrawn and isolated. Fortunately, not all teachers where like Mrs. Kelly and my new teacher was wonderful. Mr. Glenn was a kind man and recognized the mess he had inherited when it came to me. I think he spent an inordinate amount of time and effort trying to undo the damage that had been caused by my previous years.

He probably struggled with understanding the heart of my issues, but that was because I had locked them all away. I felt that revealing the truth to anyone would result in rejection and ridicule. I had taken the precious and innocent little girl that I truly was, locked her away in an inaccessible closet, and left her alone. There she languished, away from the sight of the world. She remained unexpressed, unknown, and unwelcome. Never did the sunlight touch the recesses of the dungeon where I had placed my true self. Still, Mr. Glenn tried to reach me anyway he could.

One day as I was drawing, he stopped at my desk and looked down at my picture. I was afraid I might be in trouble for not focusing on more important assignments. He took the picture and raised it to examine it closer." This is really good." he said, in a surprised tone. I said nothing but I looked around the room hoping that the other students hadn't noticed. After that, he tried to draw me out using this gift. As often as he could, Mr. Glenn encouraged my drawing and even excused me from some class activities in order to let me do something I truly loved. Of course, he insisted upon my completion of other classwork, and never neglected a balanced and wholistic approach to my education.

He also encouraged my writing. My ability to write was hampered by the fact that we were often required to present our creations to the class. The very idea of standing before the other students and reading, petrified me. Consequently, I rarely completed any assignments in this discipline. Instead, I opted for low grades in anything that was related to English, including writing.

I must have been one of the most frustrating students of his career. To see such marvelous potential utterly wasted had to be heartbreaking for him. Perhaps he knew about my IQ test, or maybe he was just able to detect so much more than others could see. I think he truly cared for all of his students, but with me, it was as if he was trying to save me from my apparent fate and ultimate oblivion. I think he knew how close I was to drowning in a life of darkness and sorrow, but I so often refused the lifeline he offered me.

I remember on so many occasions when he pleaded, "Jody, I know you're smart enough to do this. This should be easy for you".

"Why won't you even try?", he asked.

My response was similar every time. I averted eye contact, shrugged my shoulders and sometimes mumbled in a low tone, "I don't know."

He was not a man who gave up easily, and he truly never gave up on me. On several occasions he asked for specific drawings. He sometimes allowed me to sit on the floor in the back of the classroom and draw to my heart's content. I liked him very much and because of this, I complied with his requests. Drawing seamed much safer than writing because once the creation was done, it required no explanation. I didn't have to talk about it.

I found the activity extraordinarily peaceful and pleasant. It removed me from the attention of the other students for a time and permitted my day dreams to take shape on the paper in front of me.

I could be in my own world and I expressed the beautiful imagery of my imagination. Of course, I couldn't express all of my inner thoughts. That would have been a disaster. I was careful to never draw anything that was too girly, so images of flowers, unicorns or rainbows were never indulged.

As Christmas approached, Mr. Glenn gave me an assignment that became a turning point in my life. He asked me to draw some really big pictures of Elves, Santa and his reindeer and other Christmas related Art. I gleefully accepted the challenge and tried to do a reasonable job.

Once the Christmas pictures were completed, Mr. Glenn rolled them up carefully and took them away. His mysterious actions made me nervous. I guess I had never really thought about what would be done with them once they were finished. I didn't have to wait too long to discover the location of my 5th grade masterpieces.

The next day, Mr. Glenn informed me that my art was to be featured in some of the local merchant's windows on Leadville's main street. I was mortified. I tried so hard to never be noticed by anyone. It was my desire to "sneak" through life unseen and anonymous. But this was terrible! "How could he do this to me? I trusted him." I groaned to myself. "Now everyone will see them." I screamed in my mind. "Oh God, don't let this happen." I prayed silently.

He must have seen the terrified look on my face, so he put his hand on my shoulder and said, "This is a good thing, Jody. Trust me. You'll see." As he walked back to his desk, I sat there thinking, "Trust you! How can I trust you! Do you know what you've done to me?"

The day passed intolerably slow. All I could think of was finding a rock to crawl under. It didn't matter that he considered such attention positive. It was notoriety in my mind, and that was simply unacceptable.

When I returned home, I discovered to my horror, that my parents already knew about the public display of my work. They were very excited and anxious to go for a drive to see my pictures prominently displayed. I felt exposed and terribly vulnerable, but I tried not to let on. So, into the car we went and began the embarrassing drive to go see what their child had accomplished.

I could see the pictures in the front windows of the businesses as we drove by. Dad stopped the car and we ventured down the sidewalk to see the displays up close. I swiveled my head constantly looking for classmates I hoped would never materialize. My parents were so proud of me, but my paranoia robbed me of the joy of that moment.

On the drive home, they repeatedly praised me and expressed their pride. Although I didn't enjoy the attention, it was obvious that my parents were joyful. That helped me feel better about the whole thing. Still, I dreaded having them noticed by my classmates.

The next day at school, one of the girls in my class approached me and said, "Hey Jody, my parents saw your pictures." I braced for the mocking that I was sure would come. But to my surprise, she added "Pretty cool."

During the following days, I began to feel differently as fellow students offered only praise and complements. I was still embarrassed, but I started to feel like there was something good about me. "Maybe, I'm not a total looser." I thought.

Mr. Glenn was right. He knew exactly what he was doing and what I desperately needed. For the first time in my young life, I started to feel the stirrings of self-esteem. I even permitted myself to dream larger, happier dreams once again. I didn't always have to fantasize about dying. I could once again dream the dreams of the living.

I permitted myself to feel good about some aspect of myself. I sometimes imagined myself pursuing a career as an accomplished artist. Although I still avoided personal attention, I enjoyed the attention my artwork received.

Once during an art exhibit featuring local students, I anonymously meandered through the crowd and delighted in the positive comments I overheard while eavesdropping. Since I had achieved virtual invisibility, it amused me every time I heard people trying to figure out who the artist was. They repeated my name, but had no idea I was standing next to them as they admired my work.

I never became a professional artist, but the praise that my art solicited went a long way toward helping me feel some measure of worth. Mr. Glenn had finally cracked the shell in which I hid. I regret the fact that I never properly thanked him for his kindness and his belief in me. He was the most influential teacher of my young life and through his effort and determination to help me, I began to heal. I still felt terrible about who and what I was. I didn't value myself, but I began to value the things I could create. Art was only one aspect of this. It was about the same time I discovered the world of modeling.

I had always been obsessed with flying because of the freedom it represented. When I was younger, I often prayed that God would turn me into a bird. Then I could fly away from the bullies in time of need and even imagined I'd remain a bird and leave the world of people and pain far behind. When I got old enough to realize I'd never be a bird, aircraft took over the "flying away" fantasy. I didn't understand how helicopters worked, so I focused on balloons I had seen on The Wizard of OZ and other shows. My love of balloons and kites eventually changed to a love of airplanes.

During this time, I was introduced to model airplanes by my uncle who had quite an extensive collection. Even though the detail he put into his creations was amazing, they were the heavy plastic kind which were great for looking at, but not useful for anything else.

As fate would have it, my science teacher had constructed a large balsa wood bi-plane that had a five-foot wingspan. It not only flew, but could be controlled by a small handheld device through radio waves. When I remember those days, I smile given the extensive proliferation of drones available to the public now. However, the technology he demonstrated was amazing to a child in the 1960s, and I was hooked.

I think for me, the fact that he had constructed such a large model that could fly, gave rise to the idea, that perhaps one day I could make one large enough to take me to safety.

I developed a love of balsa wood model airplanes. At first, I focused on the ones that used a rubber band to power the propeller. This progressed to small aluminum engines and eventually model rockets.

Modeling had another advantage. It was a "boy thing". That idea wasn't lost on me. In fact, it was nice to do something that I enjoyed that others saw as masculine. I hated sports and didn't even know how to talk to guys about the things they liked. Building models was something I could do and enjoy, and I became good at it.

I spent many hours in my bedroom building the small flying devices, and always fantasied about larger versions that would one day permit me to fly away from my life. I had no destination in mind when I imagined my escape. I simply felt that anywhere would be better than here, and any life was better than mine. Starting over as someone else, had its appeal. Sometimes I'd think about the phrase I had heard on TV, "sex change". I never said it out loud, but it symbolized hope and often raddled through my brain.

Constant bullying dominated the landscape of my middle-school existence. My anxiety rose sharply whenever I was forced into the company of anyone outside my family. Of course, being a child in school made that an almost daily occurrence. To make matters worse, my parents noticed that I was floundering socially and insisted on little league baseball, bowling leagues and encouraged my participation in various sports.

I did OK with bowling, but little league and other team sports were a disaster and served only to make fellow team members hate me more. I was usually the one costing them the game, and the way I ran, and played was embarrassingly female.

My art and my models gave me the excuse to work in my bedroom and avoid the outside world. Even though I became unbearably lonely, I preferred the safety of solitude to the painful realities of a more social life. My skill increased, and in an effort to socialize me, my parents encouraged me to enter model contests and exhibitions. I often won or placed very high in these contests. It helped with my self-esteem, but I had such a long way to go. To my parents' credit, they really tried hard to help me fit into some aspect of society. Usually, I resisted their efforts. Unfortunately, avoiding social contact was very much to my detriment.

During middle school, I came to understand that it was my behavior that caused some of my suffering. I wasn't happy about being born into a boy's body, and I knew, I couldn't change who I really was inside. But I could hide behind a convincing performance. I had seen the movie, "The Prince and the Pauper" at a school assembly. Since the poor child was able to convince the world that he was a prince, I realized that I might be able to act like a boy, and possibly convince the world that I was normal. After all, the drawings I did, weren't really dogs and horses and elves, but they looked like them. The models I created weren't real airplanes, but they flew.

So, with great determination, I began creating a "model" of a boy. It wouldn't really be me, but maybe the world would believe it was me. In a sense, this would be a robot in the image of a boy. But the person controlling it would be a girl. I would be at the controls and make sure it did everything that a normal boy was supposed to do. Since the world didn't want me and wouldn't accept me, I would give them the "Boybot".

I began this great deception by first correcting my walk. I found another student willing to give me "walking lessons" in exchange for my lunch money. I had my lunch money stolen when I was younger, but this time it was my choice. I didn't know how my walk was different, but I knew that there were frequent comments like, "You walk like a girl." Or "Why do you swish when you walk?" and even, "Are you trying to get beaten up?"

The walking lessens ended in frustration for both of us. He lacked the ability to explain what I was doing wrong, and I didn't have the ability to see myself. Even after he decided to give up on me, I kept observing how boy's move their feet and body. It took about two years to modify my walk to such an extent that it stopped being noticeably female. For years following this, I had to remind myself to "Walk like a boy!" every time I got out of the car, or rose from my desk. "Walk like a boy.", I thought. I couldn't afford to forget. Just one slip-up could cost me dearly.

The rest of my persona was much more difficult to correct. It wasn't just the walk that screamed "I'm a girl!" to the watching and judging world. It was also my facial expressions, how I talked and laughed. Even the subtilties of hand gestures and body movements gave me away.

One by one I tried to eliminate the physical signs of my inner self. Hand gestures were next, but those were quite subconscious and there were so many. When we talk, we often move our hands to express ideas and emotions. When we wave goodbye or hold our books, we reveal who we are. I learned how to carry my books in a masculine way, but the extensive hand gestures were another story.

I found that the best solution to stop my hands from doing the "wrong" things, was to keep them from doing anything at all. When I wasn't holding my books or doing schoolwork, I kept my hands in my pockets. This was possible by wearing a long green jacket purchased at a military surplus store. I never removed my coat. I kept it on at my desk, in the lunchroom and walking home. It didn't matter how warm I got, it was my armor and my security blanket. "No hands, no problem.", I thought.

Of course, changing my walk and binding my hands couldn't fix all of my behavior. I solved the facial expressions and the intonation in my voice by simply not talking to anyone. I only spoke when it was absolutely necessary. The few words I used were always carefully chosen and of course I kept my communications short and to the point.

Every time I notice a masculine trait in the boys around me, I tried hard to incorporate that into my deception. This took many years to accomplish. However, the work of creating the Boybot had begun. As the years passed, I buried my true being under layer upon layer of deception and tried to disappear from society.

I walked through the remaining years of middle school as a quiet and expressionless loner. My existence was a cold and friendless walk into sorrow and isolation. Still, it was better than the violence and rejection I had suffered so often in my tender and innocent years.

Unfortunately, there was one more thing that I needed to complete the lie I told to the world. I required one more terrible change that would finally stop the bullying and bring me "safely" into the masculine deception. This hideous process couldn't be stopped and eventually it came to turn the Boybot into the Man Machine. The next and most terrible trauma was puberty, but that was still a few years away.

It was within the confines of our small middle school that another change took place. Driven by anger and frustration I began to fight back. I wasn't very good at fighting yet, but at least I sent a message to the bullies that physical violence would result in a reciprocal action. I might not "win" the fight, but I would no longer passively accept my beatings. The bullying didn't stop, but became less frequent as other students started to understand that I could hurt them back.

One day, during lunch recess, I was approached by three bullies. One circled around behind me and pushed me forward. Jim, the largest of the three, hit me hard in the stomach which caused me to double over. "What's wrong? Got a tummy ache?", he mocked. He then grabbed the back of my coat and pulled it forward over my head cloaking me in darkness. To his surprise, my frail build allowed me to slip easily out of it leaving him holding the inside-out jacket. "Slippery.", he said angrily sneering. He threw it to the ground and came for me.

He got his second surprise as my right fist smacked hard into his nose. I was shocked and startled by what I had just done. Blood was spilling onto the white snow and spreading. It was the first time I had ever hit someone. He held his nose in disbelief and looked at his hand now completely red with the warm sticky liquid. Now enraged, he let out a frightening, loud scream and came after me again. This time I felt his teeth cut my knuckles as I continued to throw determined but un-skilled punches at my assailant. The other two boys tackled me and he landed one good punch breaking my nose before I could roll to my side and protect my face. I threw the other kids off and stood up swinging once again. We all just stood there in utter disbelief. Blood was pouring from both of our noses and Jim's lip was split open. I stood there with fists at the ready, not knowing what would come next. Just then, Jim looked to his left with wide eyes and I realized a teacher was steaming our way. It was Mr. Glenn.

I sat in the principal's office feeling a different kind of shame. I had hurt someone. I had deliberately tried to cause another person harm and it didn't sit well with me. Before long Dr. Richards came in and sat down at his desk.

"I've never seen you in here before.", he started.

"No Sir." I responded quietly, barely making eye contact.

"Well, I know you didn't start it, did you?", he asked.

Once again, I responded with, "No Sir."

"Are you OK?", he probed.

"Yes", came out of my mouth, but I started to squeak as I fought back the tears.

"Well, looks like he learned his lesson, but you should get that nose looked at.", he continued.

"Yes, Sir." I groaned, as I wiped away the tears carefully avoiding the swollen and tender nose.

"Why are you crying, Jody." Dr Richards asked.

"Because I don't like hurting people." I wined through uncontrol-lable sobs.

He paused a long time looking at me with compassionate eyes and said, "I wish all of my students were as kind as you, Jody. But you've got to toughen up. What you did today, you had to do. Do you hear me?"

"Yes Sir." I whispered as I composed myself.

"Alright, get out of here, I'm sending you home for the rest of the day."

Surprisingly, Dad was home when I arrived. He looked at my red-stained shirt and asked, "Is that your blood.", in a very serious tone.

"Not all of it, Sir." I responded in and almost militaristic tone. He seemed pleased that I hadn't just been a punching bag. He folded the paper, sat it on the end table and said, "Let's go get your nose set."

The drive to the doctor's office was a long one and my dad spared me any retelling of the fight. I was grateful and quiet the whole time. The pain of having the doctor trying to put my nose bones back into place was almost more than I could bear. Still, I repressed my screams as tears flowed down my cheeks. "Making your eyes water I see.", Dr Leonardi joked.

"Yes Sir, I grunted." As the pops and crackling noises in my face continued.

Eventually, we returned home after the doctor was unsuccessful at straightening my nose. Dinner, TV and bedtime preparations passed like it was any other day. As I sat on the edge of my bed, I noticed my sister was already asleep. She had left one of her Barbie dolls on the table between our beds. I picked it up and indulged the sadness within me.

I noticed the tiny features of her face and contrasted that with my now "splattered" and swollen nose. I stroked the long hair and rubbed the stubble of my own head. My fingers felt the satin dress my sister had placed on the doll. I admired the slender shape of the dolls body and her bright eyes and bubbly face. Then I placed her back on the table and gently placed my battered face and sore nose on the pillow.

I let the tears fill my eyes once more as I stared at the Barbie. Something inside the deepest part of my soul broke as I said goodbye to the little girl within me. And like so many nights before, I cried silently waiting for sleep. Barbie was still smiling as she stared at the little girl who looked like a badly beaten boy. I continued soaking the pillow with liquid sadness until I slept.

In the weeks and months that followed, the verbal abuse continued and became even more extreme. I never started a fight over something that was said. In fact, I never started any fight. My new found toughness did nothing to stop the ridicule and name calling. Even though I was able to prevent the physical damage, the injuries to my soul continued.

Fire and Blood

THE SCHOOL I was attending was actually an old apartment complex that had been converted to classrooms and such. The "Gym" where they tried to have physical education classes was a long room with two doors. It was about the size of a hotel room, but not as nice. Even the cafeteria was a temporary building that had double doors installed to bring it up to code. This was in case we needed to run from a fire or something.

I didn't mind walking between the buildings. In fact, almost every class was in a different building. It not only gave me breaks in my day, but allowed me to wear my coat most of the time. Since I was either warming up from being outside or getting bundled up to go out again, the teachers never required me to remove my coat. My winter coat became a security and my suit of armor. I was only told to take my coat off for science class and P.E.

One cold day in the fall just after Halloween I was walking to the distant trailer where science class was held. This was one of my favorite classes. I loved science. It fascinated me and gave me a sense of wonder about the world. Everything about Science class was exciting and fun, but that was about to change.

I don't remember the assignment that day, but it involved burning things. Since the trailer wasn't set up with natural gas, we were given alcohol burners. They were small glass bottles about the size of a baseball, with a cotton wick coming out of the top. Two by two we were called to the front of the class to get our burners.

As I walked up to the front, someone on my right said, "Here, Jody, I've got an extra one." As he held out the clear glass globe, I Innocently took the bottle filled with alcohol. I knew something wasn't right when I felt my hand become soaked and the cold alcohol covered my hand and spread up my arm to the elbow. I noticed a large crack running the full length of the bottle and realized it was leaking. In fact, the leak was so bad, it was almost pouring out. I noticed my white cotton shirt was soaking up the icy liquid.

Panic gripped me as I saw him hold his own burner up to light mine. I tried to jerk my hand away, but I was too slow. A faint blue flame engulfed my hand, the burner and my arm. The fire didn't spread as much as it exploded. I heard a low "woosh" and felt the white-hot pain on my skin. I dropped the burner which continued to burn but didn't shatter. I thrust my hand and arm against my body trying to put it out. The alcohol was still leaking as flames quickly spread across the linoleum toward my pants. Fortunately, the teacher arrived and smothered the fire with a large towel.

When I looked at my hand and arm, I was still in blinding agony, I noticed my white shirt had turned brown the way a marshmallow does over a campfire. My skin was bright red with dozens of white blisters. Then I heard the laughter of the boys who had given me the leaking burner, and realized it was not an accident.

I stood there in shock, not knowing what to do. Being set ablaze in front of the classroom, made my face red from embarrassment. I guess I could have been angry, but I believed I deserved every hellish punishment my classmates invented.

To my surprise, the teacher, Mr. Benjamin, began to manhandle me to the front of the classroom scolding me for being so careless. He poured a sink full of water and immersed my hand and arm in it. I could hear the hateful, taunting comments shouted behind my back.

Somehow, I was deeply ashamed and felt I needed to apologize. My arm remained in the sink for the remainder of the class. As I touched the brown portions of the shirt, they crumbled and fell into the sink revealing my badly burnt arm. "Don't cry!", I told myself. "I'll never let them see my pain, or my tears.", I resolved.

Once again, I had to answer for another ruined shirt. There were many ruined shirts that I had to explain. Some were ripped, or blood-stained, but this was the first one that had been burned. I decided to tell my parents the truth, well, most of it. I never told them that they had done this horrible thing to me on purpose. In my parent's minds, it remains a childhood accident.

The scars have almost vanished, but I can still make out the remnants of what happened half a century ago. The memory has not faded, but remains fresh and painful to this day. It's too bad that the soul doesn't heal as fast as the body.

Our family never had much money. I suppose most people would have considered us poor, but it never felt that way. Mom and Dad knew how important social acceptance and belonging are for youngsters, so they made the effort to hide our financial situation from us. They didn't want us to think of ourselves as poor and we never did. Consequently, my mother would scrimp and save every penny she could in order to buy at least some articles of clothing for us that were fashionable.

With me, there was a far more serious challenge than simply being poor. I would have never wished my particular problem on anyone, not even my enemies. My "curse" was a much bigger issue than being poor, and I went to great efforts to hide my true nature from them. Still, my parents did what they could to help us fit in and fashionable clothing was part of that effort.

A few weeks after Christmas break, Mom called us into her

bedroom and presented my sister and I with two boxes. It was unusual to get a gift other than birthdays or Christmas so it struck me as odd. They might have been an early Easter present or she might have ordered them before Christmas and they had simply arrived late, but I was quite excited. When the boxes were opened, I saw the gift intended for me. There in a flimsy cardboard box was a beautiful pair of bell-bottom jeans. They had vertical stripes in blue and dark blue.

They smelled like new pants, which would be hard for me to describe, but they didn't feel like they were new. Up until this time, my jeans had always been the standard and very durable blue jeans which felt like stiff cardboard rather than anything that could be worn. They always needed to be washed a number of times before they became flexible enough to wear comfortably. One time I tried to wear my new Levi's and managed to stain my underwear and legs a dull greyish blue.

Sometimes I got dress pants that were often made of wool and were very itchy. The bellbottoms that I held in my hands were entirely different. They were soft to the touch and even though they were denim, they were pliable and turned out to be very comfy.

They were probably the nicest pants I had ever owned, and I wondered if they were too nice for me. When I tried them on, they fit perfectly? Mom wouldn't let me wear them to play in of course, but she did let me wear them around the house. That day, as I recall was a Friday, and I wore them around most of the afternoon and the next day whenever I was inside our apartment.

As I walked around, I began to feel a strange emotion, for which I had no name. Looking back, I know that what I felt once again, was the rudimentary start of self-esteem. It was similar to the feelings I had experienced with my artwork. But this time it was about the way I looked, and not just something I could do or create. I felt good about my appearance, or at least better.

I fantasized about going to school and having the other kids warm up to me because I had such cool pants. "Maybe, I could even make a friend.", I thought. Wow, having a friend would be wonderful. I even dared to dream that I might make multiple friends. I fantasized constantly about silly things like being invited to a birthday party or going to get a soda with my new friends. Or even to be invited for dinner so that I could meet my friend's families. I asked to wear the new pants whenever I wasn't outside and must have drove my mother crazy. But in truth, I think she was thrilled that I loved my gift so much.

Eventually the fateful day came for me to wear my new bellbottoms to school. I was extremely apprehensive, but also hopeful and excited. I was nervous because I always tried to blend in and not give anyone a reason to notice me. The wonderful gift that my mom had given me, made that unlikely. Still, I hoped I'd be noticed in a positive way and possibly break the cycle of social rejection and loneliness. I hoped that my lovely new britches wouldn't cause any teasing or angry responses.

I suppose you could say everything went pretty well during that morning. I even got some complements from other kids. It was something I was not at all accustom to and I wondered if they meant it, or if they were being sarcastic. It was so unusual for anyone to say something pleasant or complimentary that I didn't know how to respond. As I walked, I could feel the wide bell legs slapping against my shins which reminded me constantly that I looked pretty cool. I was nervous when lunch came, but I really believed this day would be different than the other times when lunch had brought me such pain and despair. As it turned out, it was different, but not in the way I had hoped.

As I stood in the lunch line, I notice a group of students pointing at me and whispering about something. I tried not to make eye contact, and just blend into the line. A few minutes later as the line crawled through the makeshift cafeteria, I accidently leaned against an outside door that wasn't latched. As the door behind me started to swing open, I lost my balance and almost fell. I quickly recovered and pulled the door closed. But a blast of cold air from outside blew into the room and made everyone gasp from the sudden chill. It also made me the center of attention. Unfortunately, that was all the reason they needed not to ignore me.

　　　　　　　　　　　　　　　　TEARS IN SILENCE

The other kids who had been watching me advanced quickly, as the one in the lead said, "Hey fairy, you made me cold!" Before I could react, they started kicking me. I'd been kicked dozens of times before, but this was different. When the first boot landed, I felt a searing hot pain. It was the kind of pain I didn't think a boot could inflict. They continued to kick my legs and landed several well place kicks on my shins. This was followed by a spreading warmth that I knew must be blood. I looked down and saw the slices in my beautiful new pants and the gaping cuts in my legs.

Two of the kids had inserted razors into the stitching between the soles and the leather on their cowboy boots. In that way, if they kicked someone, the skin would open and blood would flow. Where on earth two ten-year-old children had gotten such an idea I didn't know. Unfortunately, this had been their weapon of choice for me that day

I turned to get away and run, but there was no place to go. They had waited for me to be in the corner and boxed me in. I don't know how many times they kicked me, but it was done very quickly, to avoid the scrutiny of teachers. When they were satisfied, the "leader" said that If I told anyone, I'd wish I hadn't.

I had been threatened with knives and razors before, but had never actually been cut by them. It was the worst possible attack I could imagine and one that I could have never anticipated. The fact that it had happened on the first day of wearing my lovely bellbottoms made me certain that God was somehow behind the attack. I knew God hated me, but always thought he was too busy to get involved. Even at that age, the unlikely coincidence was hard to miss.

For the rest of the day, I wore the bloody pants as a symbol of my shame. As I walked back to the room, I was seen by at least two teachers. My pants were bloody and sliced in a way that made it obvious that I had been the victim of a violent attack. But, none of the adults who saw me ever questioned me about it or did anything to help. I didn't care. I was far more worried about what I was going to tell my parents.

The searing pain began to fade during the next few hours and my legs started to feel cold and sticky from the clotting blood forming scabs beneath my once beautiful bellbottoms. I wore an expression of brokenness for the rest of the day. I was far too sad to cry, but my heart wept just the same. There was no way to avoid what I knew was coming when I returned home, but it turned out to be far worse than I could have imagined.

That afternoon, my mother alternated between bursts of anger and crying. "Tell me who did this to you.", she demanded. "I don't know mom. I don't know everyone's name yet.", I said. But of course, I was lying. I knew perfectly well who my attackers were, but if there had been any conversation between my parents and theirs, the truth might come out. If that happened, my folks would realize that their son was "queer", whatever that meant.

The blood had merged with the fabric and had clotted. She was applying wet washrags to soften the scabs in an attempt to separate the cuts on my legs from the sliced pants. Each time I felt the warmth of the water spread through the badly sliced spectacle; I remembered the attack. It reminded me of the blood absorbing and spreading through the denim when I was kicked. I let her cry and suffer in front of me because I couldn't take the risk of losing my parents love. I couldn't let them discover what I was. So, I continued the deception as I watched my mom cry and struggled to remove the shredded cloth. The pain renewed itself along with the burning sensation as the cuts reopened and began to color the washrags.

I watched my mom suffer and cry in front of me. I was glad that my own pain distracted me from her tears. Deep down, I knew the source of my mother's heartache was not the ruined pants. It wasn't even the brutal attack or the vicious little monsters who had done this. I knew that the source of her pain was me. It was because of what I was. Her freak of a child had hurt her. It was my fault. I was the real monster and I wished with all my heart that she had a normal child to replace me.

This was the first time that I knew for sure that the disgusting thing that I was, had severely hurt someone I loved so deeply. I knew her heart was breaking. To know that I was the cause of my mother's sorrow tore me up inside. It would be a long time before I received any clothing that I was truly excited about. Perhaps I simply chose not to get excited about anything good. I understood how fast joy could be stolen from me. I try not to think about that time, but truly the memory has not faded over the decades. When I close my eyes and think back, I can still feel the burning slices that I endured so long ago.

∿

Just Fall Down

Junior High is such an awkward time for most kids, but for me, the three years I spent in that crucible of pain and awkwardness were a nightmare. I didn't know it, but things were about to get worse in Junior high. I entered 7th grade as a pre-pubescent 12-year-old. I was a "late bloomer". I wasn't terribly small, but I was very thin. I had slender, frail arms and legs, while other boys were developing into men. It was within this context that some of the most brutal abuses occurred. Oddly enough, it wasn't always the other boys and girls tormenting me. Sometimes, it was the adults.

I began my junior high years with an incident that still burns in my memory. A boy by the name of Peter was soon to be used by the coach to punish me. Peter was older and was already on the verge of manhood. He had facial hair, a deep voice and very muscular arms. In addition to his size and muscularity, he had spent the summer in boxing camp. Peter was a nice guy who had never bullied me. He had also never stood up for me, but that was almost universal. Standing up for such a pariah was social suicide.

One day, as we walked into the gymnasium, coach Snyder had

constructed a primitive boxing ring with some left-over wrestling mats. He had also rounded up a couple of sets of boxing gloves that were lying next to the mats. This was something totally new to me, so I must admit I was curious and interested. I had never seen boxing gloves up close.

Our class came in and sat around the perimeter of the "ring". When we were all seated, coach began to explain that since Peter was away at boxing camp for the summer, he would be showing us what he had learned. "Let's see", Coach murmured, "who's going first?", he asked as he surveyed the students. "First?", I thought. I hope we don't all have to fight. Then I looked at the clock. There was less than forty minutes before the bell and I realized coach had to allow at least a few minutes of locker-room time to change our clothes. "That's less than two minutes each and that's not enough time for everyone to have a turn.", I thought. So, I began to feel better.

Several hands sprung up from boys wanting to prove themselves but to my utter shock and horror, he called on me first. "Dungan. Get up here.", he bellowed. "I didn't have my hand up coach." I responded shakily. His face turned to a menacing glare as he growled, "Get up here now!"

We had all learned not to disagree with coach because he was perfectly capable of inflicting pain and injury. We had witnessed this on numerous occasions when boys who experienced a lapse in judgment had mouthed off, or refused his commands.

As I stood, Peter and coach took one hand each and slid the heavy boxing gloves onto my spindly arms and laced them up tight. I tried to comfort myself with the fact that they were padded. "Maybe it will feel like being hit with stuffed teddy bears.", I thought, or at least hoped. When they released the gloves, I felt the full weight and thought, "How can I fight in these." "I can barely lift them." But I had only a couple of seconds to think about it as coach reached over and rang a makeshift bell.

Peter came toward me aggressively. I was clumsy as I lifted the gloves to my face and tried to block Peter's punches. It was no use.

He landed almost every punch, and he hit me so very hard. It didn't feel like being hit with teddy bears at all. It was more like being clobbered with saliva covered leather mallets. With every punch came that familiar brain-jarring thud, cracking sounds in my ears, and the smell of wet leather.

Each time he connected with my face, it made me stumble and I had to regain my balance. I attempted to punch back, but it was woefully pathetic. When it became obvious that I could neither hit my opponent or prevent his blows, I looked at Snyder to see if there was going to be any mercy, but he was thoroughly enjoying himself. Then I noticed most of the other kids were laughing as well. I'd had enough, so I set my feet about shoulder wide. I turned toward the coach and looked him strait in the eyes as I lowered my gloves. "Hit him.", Snyder barked. Peter dutifully obeyed the coach and kept clobbering me.

I could see on Peter's face that he was horrified by what coach was making him do to me. "Harder!", shouted the coach. As the spectacle continued, I noticed Peter looking at coach with a desperate exasperation. The room was spinning and I could no longer hear sounds clearly. I thought that at any moment Peter would land the knockout blow and this torment would end. To my surprise, it continued.

Again, and again my soft, childish face absorbed the impact of the man bludgeoning me with gloves that felt like battering rams. This went on longer than I thought possible, but I kept looking at coach in utter defiance. The beating stretched on until two of the boys yelled, "Just fall down." Even though my staggering made it appear that the match would soon end, I refused to fall down, and of course coach wouldn't back down either. He and I were engaged in a battle of wills, which made the physical assault seem unimportant.

After all of the other students began chanting "Fall down, fall down." I saw the embarrassment, shame and anger growing in the coach's expression. When it finally reached a point where Snyder was filled with rage, I almost expected him to start hitting me too. But instead, he roughed me up a bit and removed my gloves saying, "You

　　　　　　　　　　　　　　　　　　　TEARS IN SILENCE

don't deserve to wear these. Get your ass to the locker room."

As I staggered to the lockers, I couldn't help feeling a sense of accomplishment. I knew in my heart, "They may break my body, and even hurt my mind by making me fearful, but my soul belongs to me." Even though Peter could have landed that knockout blow at any moment, I knew that they couldn't force me to willingly give up the last little piece of myself, and I never did.

Several years later, I spoke with Peter and he told me that, on that day he had gained a great deal of respect for me. He said, "I wasn't holding back until the very end." Then he chuckled and said, "I don't think I could have remained standing." Then he sincerely apologized for what had occurred that day. I accepted as graciously as I could even though I still felt intimidated by him. Even though he was friendly enough, the feeling of anxiety never really left me when he was around.

I understand that puberty can be an unpleasant time for most youngsters, but experiencing a puberty that does not match your inner truth is especially horrific. Imagine being a little girl, but being forced to endure a male puberty. Every day you become a bit hairier, taller, more muscular and less like a female. The deepening voice and facial hair filled me with despair. There were also, the excruciating changes in the face as my brow thickened and my Adams Apple became more prominent. I found that shaving my face was heartbreaking as I felt all vestiges of childhood being replaced by unwanted manliness. Any imagined femininity was forcefully ripped from me through my biology.

For so long other children had been my enemies, some adults became my abusers, and even God was against me. Now my own body was betraying me. It was simply too much for me to handle. So, I did the most reasonable thing I could. I buried the female Jody as deep as I could. Locked in the closet and surrounded by barbed wire, I was determined to never let the "true me" get out. It was within this context that a new Jody began to emerge. Maybe everyone was trying to help me by toughening me up for life's trials. If so, they were about to get what they wanted, but greatly magnified.

I suppose I could have become a bully myself and lashed out at the brutal world around me. I could have sought vengeance on those who had hurt me, but hatred and violence were never a part of my nature. I always felt empathy for any weaker child who had to face the cruel punishment of the strong. I could have let the world turn me into a monster, but instead, I became the antibully.

As the years ticked by, and the dreadful changes of puberty took hold, I determined that there was only one rational course of action. I had to forget about the dream of being female. Even though I knew I would never be male, I could fake it. By copying the behavior of the guys, I saw every day, I was eventually able to complete the Man Machine.

I knew that what people saw on the outside was a lie, but it was a mask that served me well for a time. I used the strength and size of this new image to protect the little girl within me, but I also used it to defend those who were so often needing a hero. After a time, the weak and defenseless in our school found in me a refuge. They feared me almost as much as the bullies, so none of them ever became my friends. But they understood that I would never tolerate their victimization so they tried to stay close whenever I was present.

I remember on one occasion as I walked through the hall with my entourage of ragged refugees. Dr. Stark, the school guidance counselor, saw us and voiced, "Who are you, Jody? The pied piper of nerds?" I looked at him and simply responded. "Yeah, something like that."

Once, while standing outside the school, a smaller child approached me and asked, "Sir, can I stand next to you while I wait for my bus?" I found the term "Sir" oddly inappropriate for an exchange between two students. It was also troubling because I never wanted to be a "Sir". I also knew that it didn't represent my inner truth. Still, I had deliberately created this avatar to represent me and protect myself and others from the behavior that so often traumatizes the young.

I looked him over and responded with, "What's up kid, you got someone after you?" He sheepishly bowed his head and said softly,

"Yeah, two guys said they were going to beat me up after school." I didn't smile, but nodded my head and answered, "Sure, it's fine, stay close."

After hearing this I saw his whole body relax and his expression changed from one of fear to one of relief. A minute or two later, the bullies showed up and started to taunt him. He didn't say anything but glanced at me with pleading eyes. I spoke in an expressionless tone like I was commenting on the weather and said, "Leave him alone."

The bullies didn't address me directly, but instead taunted him even more with, "Oooo, you gotta big tough friend now." I could tell the boy next to me was starting to panic so I squared my shoulders and took a step toward his tormenters. The terrified boy slid behind me as I issued the warning once more, but louder. My countenance changed to one of anger and menacing intent. The bright sun, now in my face illuminated my stature and my now scowling expression. Everything in my body language and demeanor shouted, "Bad shit's about to happen." The two bullies backed away and kept walking to distance themselves from me.

Before they left, one of them turned around to shout a warning at the frightened child standing near me. "You won't always have your body guard, you know!" "See you later, looser."

I looked at the small boy who was wearing an expression of relief, mix with despair about the comment. Compassionately, I reassured him with, "If they mess with you, come find me."

He stood up straight for the first time, took a deep breath and said, "Thank you."

"No problem." I responded. As I notice my bus pulling into view. "Well kid, that's my bus. You, OK?", I asked.

He franticly surveyed the approaching busses lining up behind mine. Choking fumes from the diesel-powered busses collected in the hot sun.

I had no desire to miss my ride, but I lingered as long as I could to keep an eye on my frail companion. As the correct number appeared on the otherwise identical busses, he said with great relief, "Yes, that's my bus." As he pointed, he repositioned the worn backpack, and practically sprinted to the safety of the yellow refuge.

As he neared the doors now opening to receive him, he turned to look at me once more. He didn't speak but the look on his face said more than words could ever express. As the doors of my bus opened, I smiled and whispered under my breath, "You're welcome kid."

I had begun the slow process of reintegrating into society, but the role I chose was an awkward one. I presented as the troubled loner or the strong, silent type. This turned out to attract some attention from young women. The attention they showed me was not unwelcomed. After all, dating females was the best way to dispel the rumors that I was a "faggot". It also gave me a bit of a social life which I had been deprived of for so many years.

I enjoyed the company of women but never really enjoyed the romantic or sexual side of those relationships. It wasn't that I found women unattractive, I was just so uncomfortable with the thing between my legs. Consequently, I found that sex held little interest for me. That caused some issues with my girlfriends and eventually the young ladies I dated moved on to more masculine guys.

Eventually, I married, solidified a career and had children. All of which validated the idea that I was normal and things would work out. Unfortunately, when we suppress who we truly are, the pressure can be terrible. For me, living a lie was shredding my internal life and I began to sink deeper and deeper into despair and unexpressed sorrow.

On one occasion, my daughter came into my office and told me she knew I was a tormented soul. "I don't know what the problem is" She said, "but I just want you to know I see your pain and if you ever need to talk, I'm here for you."

My response was, "Thank you, I can't really talk about it, but I could use a hug from time to time." Then I managed a sad smile. She was in junior high at the time, and I marveled at her sensitivity and insight.

I shared so many wonderful moments with my children as they grew. In fact, they were the anchor of my sanity that my parents had been when I was young. God always provided me with wonderful souls who could pull me back to the land of the living when things were tough.

ON DEATH AND DYING

THE ROOM WAS decorated with an abundance of flowers and decorations meant to give comfort and peace to those who were paying their final respects. I arrived at the funeral home late, due to the long drive from Denver. The emptiness and quiet of the room struck me at once and contrasted with the thoughts and emotions I felt. This was a man I had known all my life and I rifled through so many memories and images of the man. I approached my uncle's coffin with mild trepidation.

As I stood before the open lid and observed the contents, I thought, "That's not my uncle." Although I saw the similarity, there was not the slightest sign of life, no expression, not even the smile which he so often wore. His sparkling eyes that so often gleamed with mischief were closed and I wished I could see them once again. He was such an expressive man when he lived. But his laughter and scowls, his looks of concern and interest, were all gone. There was no doubt in my mind that the lump of flesh I gazed at was not my uncle. Still, I remained transfixed, looking at the last piece of him I would ever see.

As I stood before my uncles remains, I felt such sorrow. My sadness was not for myself or for him, it was for his wife and children. I know that we all lose our loved ones to death. But the universal commonality of the experience does nothing to lessen the pain. Each death is so deeply personal for those of us left to mourn. As an adult, I had visited him rarely, but my heart wept for his children and closest loved ones.

Then my mind fixated on a series of questions. I thought, "Did I really know him?" "Do his children really know him, or did he keep secrets locked away as I do?" "Does his wife really know the man she lived with for so many years?"

While mulling through these unanswerable questions, I stumbled upon an unbearable fact. "No one, absolutely no one knows me.", I thought. In that blinding moment of realization, I understood the most fearful truth. I said to myself, "There is not another soul on this planet who knows who I truly am." Then I finally grasped the terrible thing I had done to myself and all of the people who loved me. They didn't love me. I had never allowed them to love me or even to know me. They loved the Man Machine that I had invented so many years ago.

I had been wearing a mask all along. I was playing a part. My entire life, I had been acting in a play and performing the role that the world had assigned to me. Dutifully, I had buried the real me in that dreadful closet of long ago. I knew the little girl was still there under all of the deception. But I had locked her away and ignored her desperate cries for help.

The excruciating truth that emerged that day was simply that I had never lived. I had never actually shown up in my life. Not once had I been my authentic self. If I had died that day, it would have been exactly as if I had never existed at all.

It was then that I started to understand the ever-constant loneliness I felt. It was a loneliness I carried with me into the most festive and welcoming crowds. I have not often been depressed. But that was because I chose to focus on the joy and simple pleasures that life had to offer. But even in the midst of my most precious and joyful moments, there was a backdrop of sorrow. It was because "I" was not there. I was an observer of my life, not a participant. And with that, I understood, I don't actually have a life. I have never been me and therefore have never lived.

At this time, I was not at all convinced that I needed to transition to female. I was fortunate to be seeing a brilliant gender therapist. She was not the type of therapist that believed everyone experiencing gender dysphoria should automatically transition. She felt there were many ways a person could express the gender that they felt internally. She had such a practical approach to the whole issue and made a great deal of sense. She often suggested options that didn't involve a radical dismantling of my life. She presented me with questions such as, "Can you be happy being a more feminine male?"

It was the funeral of my uncle that convinced me that I needed to "show up" in my life. I finally knew that to be truly happy, I needed to be authentic with myself and those around me. I had recently seen a rerun episode of "Star Trek the Next Generation" entitled "Encounter at Farpoint". There was a line uttered by Capt. Picard that had an immediate and profound impact on me. The quote was:

"If we're going to be damned, let's be damned for what we really are."

It was a simple quote, but the plain truth it represented was undeniable. The quote rattled around in my brain for several months, but it was the funeral that finally revealed to me the future I needed to have.

I had "wasted most of my life trying to be what the world wanted me to be and had even had a fair bit of success in doing so. From the outside, everything looked fine. In fact, it appeared to be more than fine. I had a beautiful wife, wonderful children, a dynamic and abundant career and a healthy and attractive body. But it wasn't me. On the inside I was unraveling and suicidal, which was the reason I started seeing a therapist in the first place. I now understood that regardless of the outcome and no matter the cost, I had to use the years I had left to live an authentic life as a woman.

I returned to Denver and during the next appointment with my therapist we discussed my decision.

                                    TEARS IN SILENCE

She told me, "If you transition, you might lose everything. You could lose your family and friends, your ability to make a living and even your health or life."

"Wow." I responded and began to laugh. I pretty much knew all of this but to have it laid out so bluntly was daunting.

She continued, "I'm not saying you will lose all of those things, but you must be prepared for the possibility that you will lose everything!"

I smiled nervously and asked, "Do you warn everyone this way?"

"Yes, I do." She responded.

"Does that ever scare anyone away?", I queried.

"Not if they're truly transgender." Was her reply.

"How many years have you done this type of therapy, and how many trans people have you treated?", I asked.

"Almost thirty years." She responded reflectively and added, "And I've treated more people than I can count."

"And no one has ever backed out?" I queried once more.

"Not one.", She said.

"Well, I think you and I both know that if I don't do this, I'll suicide.", I said, as a matter of fact.

"That's my assessment as well, Jody. How would you like to proceed?"

And with that, I knew she would provide one of the letters necessary to continue my remarkable journey. She also got in touch with another gender therapist and made an appointment for me to get a second opinion and the final letter needed to present to the surgeon. Shortly after this, I began the required step of living fulltime for a year as a female.

To compare transition to death is not such a reach, especially for those who have built a life. Even if that life was built upon a lie, to see it all destroyed is a kind of death and rebirth. Many transgender people resonate with the image of the butterfly. The metamorphosis and transformation that takes place is so radical that the symbol is appropriate. For me however, I fixated on the phoenix.

The legend of the bird reborn through fire, felt more appropriate for my situation. The phoenix was said to go into the wilderness, build its own funeral pyre and cast itself upon the flames. It's a deliberate act of self-destruction with the hopes that something better would arise from the ashes.

I truly had no idea what the future would hold for me after the gender reassignment was complete. So, to say I was nervous would be a gross understatement. I felt I should have been more grateful for the blessings I enjoyed, but I was truly miserable. In any case, I had finally made my decision and the construction of the pyre had begun.

I could detail the process of "coming out", medical treatments, effects of hormones and the discrimination that ensued following my decision, but that would be an entire book in itself and has been well chronicled by so many others. This is intended to be an offering of an internal journey. To spend too much time on the physical mechanics would eclipse that mission. I will say that I followed all of the required protocols and timelines for such an undertaking. I encountered much opposition and discrimination during my transition, but also many wonderful people filled with compassion. Eventually, the time for the final step had arrived.

It's was a nice day for January, I told myself as I trudged up the lonely hill in front of me. I wore an unzipped winter coat which caused me to alternate between sweating and shivering. Periodically, I looked up to see the shrine, but to my disappointment, the view was obscured every time I tried to catch a peek of the small white building.

The narrow, paved road was closed to cars that day, due to snow left from the previous day. White blobs were piled on the tree branches of the short pines and cedars. They would occasionally dislodge from the wind as they melted. These clumps of white fluff made small plopping sounds on the baren earth beneath the gnarled, old limbs. The twisted grey bark on the ancient trees filled the air with the scent of wet wood. I was panting and sweaty as I reached the top and stood before the shrine.

Mom and Dad waited in the car at the bottom of the hill. We were not Catholic, but the distant sight of the Ave Maria shrine and the white cross next to it had caught my attention. When I saw the tiny pearl glistening in the sunlight, I felt a need to visit.

After reaching the top, I took in the view afforded by the slightly higher ground. I could see the hospital which sat at the foot of the hill I had just climbed. I offered prayers that day, not to Mary, but to a God I hoped was still with me. I had more reasons than most to imagine that God had abandoned me. But I retained the faith of my childhood and chose to believe the love of God was still available to me.

There had been a huge winter storm the previous day that had made the drive from Denver perilous. Consequently, what should have been a three-hour scenic drive turned into an eight-hour ordeal of squinting eyes and white knuckles. If we had been traveling for any other reason, we would have most certainly turned back. But the event that had brought us to Trinidad had been planned far in advance, purchased and was profoundly important.

We had never spent much time in this part of Colorado. The previous day's blizzard had been replaced with the sun and warmth of today. So, we indulged ourselves in some sightseeing. We had eaten at a wonderful Italian restaurant and had learned quite a bit about the history of the town as we meandered about. I think this was mostly to distract us from what loomed only a few short hours ahead.

My parents had been magnificent that day. Mom even managed to act cheerful. Soon, it was time to check into the hospital and the mood began to change. There was the usual completion of medical forms, meetings with various hospital personnel, and preparations for the following day. My surgeon stopped by for consultation and to answer any questions lingering in my mind. I'm not sure I slept at all that night. There was so much to consider, anticipate and dread that my mind raced all night long.

My parents showed up the following morning after their breakfast. I was starving and I found it peculiar that when asked, they had a hard time recalling the meal consumed only an hour before. Now, when I consider everything that they must have been going through that day, I don't find it at all odd.

I was being prepped for the day's events. My mother retained her calm and reassuring demeanor, but Dad had become stoic and quiet. Eventually, he stood before me and said "I love you, and I'm here for you if you need anything, but I'm going to wait in the car." As he spoke, I noticed tears welling up in his eyes and knew he was grieving the loss of his only son. I wished I could have spared him this sorrow, but I also knew that he was mourning the loss of someone who had never really existed. I expressed my love and tried to reassure him, but I understood that this was something he had to work through on his own.

In truth, my parents did lose their son that day. My children also lost their father. And, there were friends and family that I would never see again. Although I regretted being the source of so much sorrow and loss, I knew it was the pain that comes from ending a pleasant deception. Truth is often harsh, but also precious and pure.

I find it strange that when we consider the act of changing one's gender, or having a "Sex Change" as they once called it, we think only of the surgery. We rarely consider all of the steps that lead up to this point. I had been on hormones for quite some time and completed the required steps with my therapist. I had gone through the "Real Life Test", suffered through electrology, obtained letters of recommendation etc. However, it is the finality and symbolism of this step that looms so enormous in our minds.

As the moment approached, I found myself with my mother and one of my dear friends, Renee. I was already relaxed from the Valium they had given me a short time ago. Just before they left me, Renee spoke words that felt like they had come from the heart of God. "Just think" She said, "You're going to go to sleep and when you wake up, you'll be a girl." I was reminded of those times so many years ago, when a four-year-old had knelt by her bed and asked God for a miracle.

I remained on the gurney as the nurse made final preparations and

                                    TEARS IN SILENCE

started wheeling me down the hall to surgery. With the distant beeping and sporadic soft noise in the hospital, I marveled at Renee's words. I smiled and even chuckled to myself as I thought, "How about that, God does answer prayers." It's not always in the way we think, or according to our timeline, but God really does perform miracles.

As my small cotton covered "ship" arrived through the double doors and I was greeted by the medical staff and the bright welcoming lights, I felt gratitude. I was grateful my family had not abandoned me. I was grateful to have this life-saving procedure available. But mostly I was grateful to God for remaining with me through this arduous journey.

Finally, I had arrived at the end of my life and the beginning of a new one. As the anesthesiologist placed the mask on my face and gave me instructions, I remembered my childhood. I turned my attention once more to God, smiled and with all my heart said, "Thank you for hearing my prayers." Then, I closed my eyes.

MY SECOND LIFE

SEVERAL WEEKS AFTER my surgery, I was permitted to take a bath instead of a shower. I lit candles, played soft music and filled the tub with bubbles. After settling into the warm embrace of the gentle water, I let happiness wash over me. I noticed the floral sent and flickering light from the candles. I slid my hands along soft, hairless legs and arms. As I relaxed into the music and ambience all around me, I smiled. Gingerly, I put my hand between my legs and for the first time in my life didn't feel the distressing appendage. Finally, it was gone and my joy could not have been deeper or more satisfying. I didn't touch myself for arousal, I did it to reassure myself that the forty-five-year nightmare was over.

Since that time, my life has been joyful, satisfying and at times quite adventurous. I've known the simple pleasures of being called "ma'am" or "grandma". And I've experienced the exhilaration and giddy sleeplessness from falling in love with a man. I've traveled in Europe, the Caribbean and Asia. And I've done all of this as my true self. My life has had its challenges, but it has also been joyful and deeply satisfying.

When I think back on the days of wanting to die, I feel shame.

I'm embarrassed that I didn't always see the extraordinary gift that is life. All lives are worth living and those who have suffered are often the people most worth knowing. Life is not about pleasure or money or even social acceptance. The true glory of life is found in overcoming adversity and expressing love to those around us. To find the treasure in every loss, and the seeds of despair in every gain is wisdom.

Now I understand that every exquisite misery and heartbreaking joy are merely colors on the tapestry of existence. Our strength comes from being brutalized and resiliency is born of onslaught. The endless longing of our desires sweetens the actualized dream. Being rejected by society, only deepens our bond with nature. It is the echoing cavity of despair that is ultimately filled with joy. Finally, I see that walking through hell connects us with heaven.

I now offer thanks to the very God that I blamed for my misery. I know that for every tear I cried, he wept more. Every time I was beaten, he felt the pain. Every time I cried out in the night, he spoke to my heart, though I couldn't hear. I was never alone or abandoned as I so often imagined. In the wilderness of social rejection, I was given my family.

I can never express my deep gratitude for the support of my parents. They have shown me such love, understanding and acceptance. I'm certain that if I hadn't had such wonderful parents, I would have perished in childhood. My life has been a difficult journey, but the love and support of family has eased my suffering all along that rocky trail.

Many trans people are rejected by family and find themselves homeless youngsters. The stories of transgender youth who are abandoned when they "come out" are so tragic, and I thank God that it was not part of my story. It saddens me deeply that some self-righteous parents, reject the children they brought into this world. This is not tough love, but an act of convenience to save the parents from embarrassment. Unfortunately, those who offer love and support to trans people are often targets of ridicule and vicious attacks. Transgender people don't choose to be the way they are, and they didn't choose their parents. They are however, worthy of love.

I wish I could say that after my transition everything has been wonderful. There has been extraordinary joy and my life has become an adventure well worth living. I can honestly say I've never been suicidal since becoming female and have rarely been sad. I still occasionally wake up startled and often exhibit residual effects of trauma. However, when I examine my life in its entirety, I feel a profound sense of wonder and thankfulness. I can say without hesitation that my life has held more joy than sorrow and more love than hatred.

Unfortunately, I've experienced a lot of discrimination. I've had doctors accept me and prepare me for medical procedures only to be denied treatment once my medical records arrived. I've even had a "Do not resuscitate" placed on me without my knowledge or consent. This was especially troubling since I was in the hospital having heart problems. That particular doctor was kind and reassuring when I arrived. He sat on the edge of my bed and even held my hand to reassure me. After receiving my records, he stood on the opposite side of the room with his arms crossed and called me "Mr. Dungan". Only then did he devalue me and assess my life as not worth saving. It wasn't the same thing as attempted murder I suppose. But it was his way of saying, "If this woman starts to die, let her. On that day, he violated his oath as a healer, and rejected the opportunity to be a decent human being.

Due to the fact that I didn't change my name, job discrimination has been ongoing for me. Frequently, the only way I was able to stay employed was by hiding my history. Usually, people don't suspect that I once lived as a male, but it's a mixed blessing. Although, it enables me to obtain work, it also forces me back into the closet. There is always the fear that I'll be discovered and end up jobless once again. I focus on my work as well as I can, knowing that the truth about me lurks in cyberspace. I can lose my job from the simple act of a colleague doing a Google search. This has become an even greater threat due to social media and personal data and histories becoming more available online.

It's not always spiteful people who unveil my secret and cost me my job. One time a cherished friend discovered my history and in her exuberant support revealed my secret to others. I was let go from my job a few weeks later. She was shocked and apologetic, but I didn't blame her. She just didn't understand the deep-seated prejudice that many have regarding trans people. It wasn't the only time that friends and colleges innocently cost me my job.

Employers rarely tell you it's because you're trans, but instead say things like, "You're not a good cultural fit." or "We've decided that the position is redundant." When you do obtain employment and are then let go a few weeks later, it becomes a red flag to recruiters reviewing resumes. Consequently, the idea that "I can always find another job." Evaporates and finding the next job becomes more difficult. I've had potential employers say things like, "Wow, you've had a lot of jobs. We're really looking for someone who will stick around."

As a trans woman, I've had to contend with the bigotry so prevalent in our world, but I don't regret my decision. There has never been a single day when I felt my transition was a mistake. The joy of finally being myself eclipses the discrimination that people throw my way. The world is changing and one day I hope that being "Trans" will not be a big deal. But for now, I navigate the prejudice and bigotry as best I can. But even on the hard days, when I'm broke and jobless my heart is often smiling.

There has been an abundance of pain in my life, but I have suffered far less than some. My heart breaks when people confide in me and share their tales of sorrow. Women have trusted me regarding continual sexual abuse and rape. Many have shared truly heart-rending tales of physical and emotional abuse in childhood. I even had a colleague who grew up an orphan in war-torn Beirut.

It is our collective shame that so many spend their lives recovering from childhood. But, it's the shining jewel of our species that many do overcome the darkness of the past. I was able to survive and even thrive, but unfortunately, many don't. Teen suicide is common among those who suffer social calamity due to sexual orientation and gender identity. Suicide is the leading cause of death for trans people and hovers at around forty percent.

Often, people endure this condition their entire lives and never transition or kill themselves. I remember a warm sunny day in Denver. I stood on a street corner waiting for a taco. The sounds of the city summer and the delicious smell coming from the food vendors made me glad to be alive. As I waited and looked around at the people and sights of the city, I notice a man in a cowboy hat staring at me from a nearby bench. He had a long bushy mustache and was dressed like he had just gotten off his horse after a cattle drive. His face was well worn and he was perhaps in his 60s but I can't be sure. He reminded me of cowboys I had worked with during my high school years.

His intense stare made me very uneasy. I had only started my transition and it was easy for people to see my awkwardness. I avoided eye contact hoping he wouldn't cause a scene or become violent. To my dismay, stood up and began to saunter over to me as my heart began to race. When we stood eye to eye, he leaned in, and with a gravelly voice, whispered, "I wish to God I had the courage you have."

He looked me in the eye once more and I saw the sorrow he had caried with him for so many years. I then realized that he was trans, just like me, but would probably never transition. He turned and sadly walked away. As I watched him disappear into the crowd, I understood that he could have been me. It was then that I looked at the dress and short heels I wore that day with renewed pleasure and gratefulness. I looked at the sky and quietly said "Thank you."

I never saw him again and I have no idea what became of him. But I suspect, he finished the rest of his life still fearful of the truth he kept buried.

A relative through marriage, told me about the death of his father. This young man had lost his dad to suicide. He explained how nobody knew that his father had been transgender until they found the final letter he left behind. In the note he explained that he had struggled with gender identity his entire life but was not strong enough to endure

　　　　　　　　　　　　　　　　　　TEARS IN SILENCE

the shame and embarrassment of transition. He chose to end his life instead.

It's unfortunate that those who exhibit gender nonconformity find themselves the target of those who are so quick to hate. Simple rights such as using the bathroom of my choice and being allowed to marry the person I love are threatened by the fearful and willfully ignorant. As gender expression takes the stage on an ever-shifting social landscape, fear often leads to anger and violence. We can choose not to see gender variance as a problem, but rather as an expression of the dazzling diversity that God has created.

Even though I count myself among the followers of Christ, I find the behavior of many in the church a continual source of frustration. Our faith preaches that God judges hearts and minds. Why then do so many resort to citing the body as proof that the heart and mind are wrong? If we are told that a person's inner truth differs from their biology, why is the most common rebuttal the supremacy of the flesh over the spirit? Is that not the opposite of what we profess?

We no longer perform exorcisms on epileptics or autistic children. We don't tie a child's left hand behind their back to force the use of their right hand. We recognize that there are conditions at birth that affect behavior but we no longer equate them with sin or demonic influence. Tragically, when a child is born gay or trans, we often judge them, condemn them and sentence them to social Hell. It was Jesus who told us not to judge, but those words are too easily ignored. It's my fervent hope that one day, compassion will lead us to behave differently. When a child, with trembling hands, offers the most intimate secrets of their heart, accept their gift, believe them, and for God's sake love them.